Seven Steps to a Successful Career

SAGE was founded in 1965 by Sara Miller McCune to support the dissemination of usable knowledge by publishing innovative and high-quality research and teaching content. Today, we publish over 900 journals, including those of more than 400 learned societies, more than 800 new books per year, and a growing range of library products including archives, data, case studies, reports, and video. SAGE remains majority-owned by our founder, and after Sara's lifetime will become owned by a charitable trust that secures our continued independence.

Los Angeles | London | New Delhi | Singapore | Washington DC | Melbourne

SAGE Study Skills

Seven Steps to a Successful Career

A Guide to Employability

Lucinda Becker & Felicity Becker

Los Angeles | London | New Delhi
Singapore | Washington DC | Melbourne

Los Angeles | London | New Delhi
Singapore | Washington DC | Melbourne

SAGE Publications Ltd
1 Oliver's Yard
55 City Road
London EC1Y 1SP

SAGE Publications Inc.
2455 Teller Road
Thousand Oaks, California 91320

SAGE Publications India Pvt Ltd
B 1/I 1 Mohan Cooperative Industrial Area
Mathura Road
New Delhi 110 044

SAGE Publications Asia-Pacific Pte Ltd
3 Church Street
#10-04 Samsung Hub
Singapore 049483

Editor: Jai Seaman
Editorial assistant: Delayna Spencer
Production editor: Tom Bedford
Copyeditor: Audrey Scriven
Proofreader: Andy Baxter
Marketing manager: Catherine Slinn
Cover design: Stephanie Guyaz
Typeset by: C&M Digitals (P) Ltd, Chennai, India
Printed and bound by CPI Group (UK) Ltd,
Croydon, CR0 4YY

Library of Congress Control Number: 2015953105

British Library Cataloguing in Publication data

A catalogue record for this book is available from
the British Library

ISBN 978-1-4739-1941-9
ISBN 978-1-4739-1942-6 (pbk)

This book is dedicated to Annie

Summary of contents

Contents

Contents

About the authors

Lucinda Becker is a university lecturer and works closely with undergraduates and postgraduates as they develop their professional attributes. She was the instigator of the Professional Track Scheme for students at the University of Reading. For many years she answered readers' queries about their career challenges in the *Reading Evening Post*.

Felicity Becker is a lecturer in the Further Education and Lifelong Learning sector and is involved in the training of transferable skills and in boosting employability through training. She has a portfolio career involving lecturing, running her own training company and working as a sign language interpreter. She has recently started her Master's in Education.

Introduction

Good careers are all about good decisions. Deciding on the person you are, the types of things you like to do, the sorts of people with whom you would like to work and, just as importantly, deciding on the best way to get there. Some of these decisions will be huge (should you abandon some of your brilliant IT skills because, actually, you would not enjoy a career in IT all that much?), some will be easy (so you dislike travelling a long distance to work? Avoid it!), and some will be tiny (at the end of a panel interview, should you shake hands with each panel member?).

The reason it makes sense to go with good decisions is that most of us want the best possible return for the effort we make. That means getting things right the first time, as often as you can, or being prepared to try out something new but only for as long as it takes to make the next decision.

It seems so simple: maximum reward for your effort as you forge ahead into a good career. So why does it not always feel that easy? There are several reasons:

1. Decision making is a complex process – we aim to help you break down each decision into a manageable set of choices.
2. You are under pressure – how often have you been told that you 'ought' to do something because you are good at it, or because you would please others by doing it? This guide is about you and what you want and need: it is *your career*.
3. Everyone is different – it may seem as if those around you are looking for similar rewards in a career as each other (working with people, or exciting travel opportunities, or social impact, or plenty of money); this will never mean that you need these things too.
4. Each stage is stressful, and sometimes it is downright scary. We know how that feels, and we plan to work with you in a positive decision-making process, rather than an intimidating test of character.
5. It just takes so much effort – it can seem as if you have been thinking about your career for years and years, ever since your schooldays, but now is the time to take charge. Maximum result for targeted effort: that can be your new goal.

The authors

We are a mother and daughter team who between us have decades of experience in dealing with undergraduates, further education students, adult learners and private professional clients, and in each of these situations thinking about careers has been part of the learning process. At times this has been direct (we both teach on employability courses) and sometimes less obvious (one of our key educational concerns is how to help our learners to stand tall in the careers market they have chosen).

We are passionate about employability and ensuring that our students and clients get the best deal, but we are also going to be blunt throughout this book. We know that, were you to ask a group of careers counsellors or employability experts any question about your career strategy, even with something as simple as whether to give full details of your referees on a CV, you would get at least six different contradictory answers. None of them would be wrong, but they would all be leading you in different directions and this runs the risk of leaving you confused and uncertain.

With this in mind we made one key decision before we began to plan this book. We are going to tell it like it is, from our point of view. It is rare for any careers conundrum to have a single, simple answer, so we are happy to rely on our depth and range of experience and learning and to give you clear answers whenever we can, confident that they will underpin our main goal: moving you towards a good career at a satisfying pace and without too much heartache.

Our readers

We know that you have bought this book because you need some career help, that much is evident, but we cannot know where you are in your career planning. You might be at the very outset – still studying, early in your course, and just beginning to think about what you might do later. You could be towards the end of a course and be panicking slightly. You might have completed your education a little while ago and feel as if you have missed the boat in some way, or you might be considering a career change.

Throughout this book you will find us referring to studying and to skills that you are acquiring. If study was a while ago for you, you might need to think back a bit or consider what you have done since then to boost your career prospects. If you have recently returned to study after a break, you will find guidance that is relevant to the 'new you' that is emerging as a result of that study, but we hope there is no suggestion that you should abandon the 'old you', who will still have much to offer in your current endeavours to achieve a good career.

You might already have noticed that we have referred more than once to 'a good career', rather than 'a perfect career' or 'the best career'. There is good reason for this. Although we cannot know all about you and your circumstances, we do know that this book will affect you in many ways. It will help you to shape your future and it will support you as you hone your career skills and develop strategies for success. We also hope to dispel a few myths along the way, and the idea of a 'perfect career' is one that does a huge amount of damage.

We both love our jobs. Indeed, our careers have been a pleasure throughout, from the earliest jobs (one of us mopped floors in a service station and loved the satisfaction of a job well done), through the learning curve (both of us have worked as freelance trainers and had to work out how to sell our expertise in a competitive market) and into our more settled positions (which still challenge us to increase our transferable skills base). We have thought, at each point, 'well, this is a good career so far'. That is enough; it is more than enough. We see students weekly who yearn for the 'perfect career', with no idea what this would really look like for them, and who will spend months, sometimes years, chasing 'the best career' fruitlessly, with no realisation that they are already in the best career for them at that particular moment in their lives.

How to use this book

Now is the time to be canny about your career, regardless of where you are in the process. If you are on the threshold of this adventure, you might want to read the book through in its entirety to get the lie of the land. If you are stuck at one particular point, that will be the section to go to first (the guide has been designed to be used in any order you like). You will find yourself returning to some sections time and again as you face specific challenges (such as an interview) but other sections will be less frequently visited as you develop your ideas and feel confident about moving on.

> **Remember!**
>
> In whichever order you read the book, there is one aspect of it that underpins everything we believe about how to approach employability and career planning: **THIS BOOK IS QUICK AND EASY TO USE!**

We have based this guide on a series of questions. Each question is answered briefly before we move on to a supplementary or linked question, or a whole new area. That way, you can be in control of the help you receive: a quick answer to a small query or a more extended series of answers in an area with which you are less familiar. As with everything else to do with career success, we aim to offer maximum results for your effort; you need never feel obliged to read through a whole chapter if you only have a few little queries (and some of the queries we cover are truly tiny, but we know that they can get in the way of your confidence).

The book is based on seven steps, as these are the steps we would usually suggest taking on the path to your career goal, but again we would not want to restrict the way in which you might prefer to approach this. It may be that you are in a position where you have covered Step Three, for example, and you are clear about your goals. In that case, you can simply skip over it and only return there if you begin to doubt aspects of your career plans. If you are feeling anxious about what motivates you, this could distract you from your main purpose, so you might want to go to that section of Step One first, before moving on to other sections.

Step One: Knowing who you are in the career market

Read this section now if:

- You are new to the job market, and have never thought much about career planning.
- You have a job (or have had several jobs) but would like to change what you do for a living.
- You know that you tend to see yourself through the eyes of others and would like to get a better sense of yourself and what you want.
- You want to develop your confidence in what you have to offer.
- You want to make the most of your experience.
- You are indecisive about where you want to go in your career.
- You are finding it hard to get started on your first, or next, career move.

1.1 Introduction: why does it matter?

This is, perhaps, the most difficult aspect of career planning. Indeed, it is so daunting for some that we were reluctant to put it here, at the beginning of this guide. But then we decided to be realistic about the task ahead of you: until you know who you are in terms of employability then you cannot move ahead effectively. This is not going to be the fastest leg on your employability journey, as we were reminded just this morning. One of us was called 'the tech queen' of a virtual learning environment, much to her surprise. In our enthusiasm to get on with the job in hand, teaching students, we have both acquired skills and experience without necessarily reflecting on the fact that this is happening. She is unlikely to go for a job at an IT call centre, but it is something that, after that stray comment, is going straight on her CV ready for her next appraisal.

Our point is that all of us change and our skills and experience evolve as we go along. Your task at the moment (and at any future points when you are making career choices) is to capture an image of the person you are in terms of your employability. This needs to be a well-rounded image; not just what do you have to offer, but what do you expect in return? Not just what could you do, but what would you prefer to do? Successful employees, those worth investing in, are people who have found a good fit between the people they are and the roles they are fulfilling. That means knowing yourself well in a career context.

Remember!

One function of a career is to make you happy. Happiness is a complicated concept but a good rule of thumb is: if you feel uncomfortable about the person you are presenting to the job market, go back and rethink before you take the next plunge.

Context is all-important here. The employability image you have of yourself will become more clearly defined as you work through this section, but it is not going to be the same as the image others have of you when they think of you as a friend, or a team mate, or a relative. Although you will bring aspects of these 'selves' to your current challenge, your career self will be different in some respects from any of these. That is not to say, though, that those who know you in those roles cannot be of great value. As well as using this guide, we will be prompting you from time to time to get some feedback from relatives, friends and colleagues.

An accurate image of yourself will be complicated – usually in a good way – by your experience. Again, there is no need to assume that the view others have of you (your friends all recall your great time on holiday last year) is the only self you have to offer. As you work through this section you will gain a better sense of which experiences you would like to promote and which you would be happy to leave behind. It is a similar story with your motivation. You might be hugely competitive in a quiz team but would prefer to work by consensus in a workplace team. As you evaluate all of these aspects of yourself, a clearer image of your work self will emerge and that will lay a firm foundation for the task ahead of you.

> **Remember!**
>
> The person anyone else thinks you are is not a complete picture of who you are in the career market – self-awareness is important in these early stages.

In this, the first step on your journey, we will aim to walk you through the ways in which you can get a clear image of yourself in the career market by answering common questions about the process. We will be looking at six distinct topics: personality, experience, qualifications, qualities, motivation and worth.

1.2 My personality and preferences

What is 'my personality at work'?

Your personality at work will have been crafted by the people with whom you work. Each colleague will have found out some part of you that contributes to an overall picture of who you are. The first impressions that were made about you were well within your control and you may have had other opportunities to present the polished 'work you'. However, we must accept that sometimes we let slip a part of ourselves that we did not intend to show; these moments may be during a stressful time when you feel at the end of your tether or during moments of delight when you have finally worked out how the photocopier works! At this stage, you may find that your personality at work is wildly different from your private personality or you may find it is very similar. The further we move away from our 'true selves', the more tiring it is to sustain an image. If you have to change your personality a huge amount to be able to fit into a job, you may need to consider a whole new career.

How can I tell how near my work self is to my true self?

The more you look into this, the more you will notice that there is not really any 'true self' for any of us, but rather the series of people we are in different contexts. Later on, we will be talking about personality tests that can help you work out what styles of working might suit you best, but it would help you to know whether the way you are working now (either in the workplace or study situation) is true to how you would like to work. There are signs you could look for that might suggest you are not working in a way that suits you (see Exercise #1 at the back of this book).

How can I get a better picture of my career self?

To get a better picture of your career self, find the time to search for evidence of how you are perceived at work (see Exercise #2).

It may be that your colleagues believe you to be very calm in difficult situations and yet you feel that you tend to panic in the same situations. Do not worry – this is very good information to have as it means you have just learnt that you are extremely good at appearing calm, even in situations that have you worrying in the middle of the night. This does not necessarily mean that you find it comfortable using this skill all of the time but it is lovely to know that you can do it.

Who can help with self-review?

You may have heard of a 360-degree review. In this you get feedback from your subordinates, your peers and your supervisors, to which you add self-evaluation. The purpose of this is to get a well-rounded review of your work and your professional development, and to be able to set realistic targets.

Although there might be systems within your workplace where you can get feedback, what should you do if you are not in work?

Well, you will be pleased to know that you can undertake the same process using the people around you.

Think about getting opinions from people in your inner circle such as your best friend or a close family member (the inner circle). Go on to get feedback from those who are on the next circle out, such as friends, and then get feedback from old colleagues, tutors and those people who do not know you so intimately (the outer circle). This will give you some idea about the qualities people see in you. You probably do not want your new employer to know that you are a fan of horror films or that you cried during the latest romantic film you watched. However, you are starting to build up a picture of yourself and you can then decide which parts of you will make up the 'career personality' that you will use.

> **Remember!**
>
> You need to get as many views as you can if you are to craft a realistic sense of who you are in the workplace or study situation, but it is easy here to lose the wider sense of yourself. Take time during the process to reflect on what you are learning about yourself, and keep notes on what you think of what you are learning. That way you can keep control of the process rather than trying to become what you think you should be, or mourning the loss of who you thought you were.

Where can I find an honest opinion for self-review?

There are some pitfalls to asking for an assessment of your personality from a wide range of people. Your friends and family, for example, see you in informal, social settings and will not want to offend you. At the opposite end, your manager or supervisor may not know you well enough to give you a well-rounded opinion. The best thing to do is to ask opinions from people you trust and respect and then piece together the commonalities. If most of the people you ask state that you are 'conscientious' then you can be fairly sure that this is an accurate assessment of your personality.

> **Remember!**
>
> One of the most difficult things to do can be to be honest with yourself, but you need this honesty to gain an accurate picture. This will help you to be successful in your chosen career.

What external tests might I do?

There are many personality tests out there. A useful one to complete is the Myers Briggs personality test as it is often used by professionals and you can access this at www.myersbriggs.org

You may also find the following websites helpful (see page 38 for more information about these): www.humanmetrics.com/cgi-win/jtypes2.asp and www.personalitypathways.com/type_inventory.html

There are other tests that you may be asked to do and so it can be reassuring to find out a bit more about them. The Belbin test is one that looks at which role you would play within a team or organisation. If you would like to find out more see www.belbin.com/rte.asp

RIASEC is another personality test and the acronym stands for 'realistic', 'investigative', 'artistic', 'social', 'entrepreneurial', and 'conventional'. You will be given an acronym that suits you at the end of the test and you can click on a link to look at the types of jobs that may suit you. You can complete this test at http://personality-testing.info/tests/RIASEC.php

Careful!

We are suggesting some websites that will give you reliable information on psychometric tests, but these can be expensive to undertake. There are three ways to approach this: pay the money, trawl through the internet until you find free options, or go along to an interview for a job that you would be happy to take but that is not your completely ideal job and take the tests as part of that process, then ask for a copy of the results.

You may choose to practise aptitude tests online, but it is important that you use a website that you can trust. Try to avoid giving out your personal details as you could end up with a lot of unwanted emails and, finally, practise the tests that you believe you are likely to be asked to undertake in your interviews. There is not much point in taking lots of numerical aptitude tests if the job you are going for does not involve mathematics!

What is the difference between an aptitude test and a psychometric test?

There is sometimes confusion over these terms, as they tend to be used interchangeably or inaccurately on some websites. Although we are offering you definitions here, do not be thrown by seeing the terms used in an unexpected way from time to time.

A psychometric test allows you to consider your personality so as to establish whether you are suitable for a role and whether that role is suitable for you. There will be a series of questions to find out what type of personality you have. This is something that we highly recommend you do yourself when searching for a new career and we will look at this in greater detail in the next question.

Top tip

Be honest so there are no inconsistencies in your results. You will ultimately be happier in a job resulting from an honest test as the job will suit you and you will suit it.

An aptitude test is used to measure your abilities and skills. This type of test is used by employers seeking an employee who will be able to pick up new information quickly and understand it well enough to utilise it. An aptitude test may involve problem-solving tasks, verbal reasoning skills, riddles, teamworking skills, non-verbal reasoning, lateral thinking tests, numeracy, literacy or computer skills. There are many websites that you can use to practise these types of tests. In some cases it can be a very narrow test allowing you to prove that you have the skills you claim to have. If you are working outside of your home country, you may have to do a language test.

Top tip

There are job agencies and some large organisations that will allow you to practise aptitude tests before you take them under exam conditions as part of the selection process. This can be a good way to boost your confidence and check that you are applying at the right level for your skills. If you miss by a small margin this might not matter and should not put you off completely, but if you take the test and fail it by a significant percentage, it will allow you to think again before spending time and effort going for a job. For an example of this, see www.gov.uk/civil-service-fast-stream-how-to-apply

Can there be a 'wrong' personality for a career?

The short answer is 'yes'! If everyone were the same, life would be very boring. You may have already had a job that you felt did not suit you and we hope that you left knowing that it was not your fault things did not work out. Equally, it is nobody else's fault. We all have a variety of skills and personality traits that will suit careers more or less, and the sooner we realise this and remove any sense of blame, the easier it is to target careers that are appropriate for us. The further we move away from our true personality and values, the harder we will find the job. One of us taught an accountant who had spent the majority of his working life in this field because he was 'good with numbers'. By the time he was 40, he was exhausted. At first he blamed it on the commute, but working from home did not give him more energy. Then he blamed it on the workload, but going part-time did not help him recover his enthusiasm. Finally, he gave it up. Now he works as an author and spends far more time in this pursuit than he ever did as an accountant. One might cynically assume that it was just the process of making a change that brought on this new-found vitality. However, five years on, with a reduced income and a young family demanding his attention, he still feels that he has more energy and less stress than when he was an accountant.

Remember!

When you are getting tired of searching for your new career, remember that it is far more tiring being in a career to which you are not well-suited.

If I suspect my current situation is not right for my personality, should I change straightaway?

Not necessarily. One of us once worked as a bookkeeper for a computer software sales firm. The work was not objectionable, but it was quite a lonely role and she discovered that the whole firm stayed behind most evenings and socialised in the office until 7pm. She wanted to scream as the clocked ticked past home time, but stayed in the job for six months because she was earning twice as much as she had in her previous job. One day, she just stood up and walked out. Not an approach we would recommend, but the point of the anecdote is that although the job did not suit her temperament, she chose to stay there for many months because, at the end of that time, she had enough money for her next training course.

Should I do some tests before I apply for a job?

Yes, this will prevent you from applying for jobs that will lead to you being unfulfilled and worn out.

Can I beat a psychometric test?

A psychometric test is rather useful and you should not see it as something to 'beat', but consider it to be a helpful way of establishing whether a particular career might suit you or not. It is best to answer honestly and calmly. Do not panic if you cannot complete some of the tests within the allotted time; this is normal for some tests, so it is best to remain calm.

People tend to think of psychometric tests as no more than a tool for a potential employer to rate you; in fact, this is far from the truth. By taking a test you are taking control of your future because it allows you to see whether you are likely to be right for the job as much as it shows the employer whether you are a good fit. It is part of a process of empowerment that can only benefit you in the long term.

Do I have to do any test I am given in the selection process?

You never have to do anything that you do not feel comfortable doing unless you understand the reasons for it. You may be asked to do some odd things during interviews, and as long as you can see why they are asking you to do something, then you should try to go along with it. If you are uncertain, then ask your interviewer to explain the reasoning behind the activity. Some organisations will deliberately set up activities to check a candidate's response to bizarre instructions. One way of testing whether candidates have a good sense of decorum and professional behaviour is to ask them to do something unprofessional and see if they turn it down. This may seem like a cruel and dishonest way of interviewing candidates and so we go back to the first sentence in this paragraph: you never have to do anything that you do not feel comfortable doing unless you understand the reasons for it.

Does the employer have to tell me which tests I will be given?

No, but you would be amazed at how infrequently candidates ask the question. Later, when we offer you advice on interviews, we will be urging you to check the location and the structure of the day; if you are to give an interview presentation you will expect to get all of the details in advance. Why not take the same approach with tests? Ask, well in advance of the interview or selection day, whether you will be required to undertake any tests, and if it seems reasonable to you, ask also whether you can be given some practice tests so you can prepare thoroughly. Even if you are not given the chance to do a practice test, this will clearly show that you are committed to the process, ready to prepare thoroughly and determined to impress.

What if I get flustered doing tests?

The old adage 'practice makes perfect' may not always be accurate, however it certainly will give you confidence going into a test. If you know that tests fluster you then take time to run through practice interviews and practice tests.

Success checklist

Here are a few ways to calm down before a test or interview:

✓ Wiggle your toes.
✓ Remove your tongue from the roof of your mouth (it got stuck up there when your mouth became dry, so a sip of water will also help).
✓ Smile. People will smile back, and even if you are alone, it will send a signal to your brain that everything is okay.
✓ Take a breath and raise your shoulders to your ears. Hold this for a few seconds and when you exhale, drop your shoulders.
✓ Think of one thing that makes you happy in life. This could be a person, a piece of music, a sunny day. Whatever you choose, this exercise will help you realise just before you have to focus on the test that this is not so big in the grand scheme of things.
✓ Check the time as it is reassuring when you can tell yourself that in an hour, this will all be over with.

Remember!

Having a relaxation technique to hand is valuable to you in all sorts of situations, so mastering this now would be wise. We are so convinced of the importance of relaxation that there is a similar but slightly longer version of the technique offered in the later section on interviews.

Is there a timeline I can use to help prepare for a test?

Yes – the success checklist below will help you to prepare:

Success checklist

✓ A week before the interview or test look through all of the paperwork you have about the organisation. This may include correspondence with the organisation, your own research on it or details you have about the test. Plan your journey there and make a note of when you need to leave your home to get there.

✓ Try not to think about it again until two days before. At this point, review the details again, to make sure that you are ready.

✓ The day before, do your best to relax by doing something to take your mind off of it; it is often our nerves that trip us up.

✓ The day of the interview or test: arrive early enough that you can look around you and relax, knowing you are ready. This also looks good to the potential employer because you have made the effort to be there before your interview or test time. You want to be there about 20 minutes early: any more and you will lose your energy as your adrenaline subsides, any less and you will be worried about arriving on time.

✓ Whilst you wait, use the relaxation techniques we have offered you.

What if I do not understand the instructions?

Firstly, do not panic. If they are written instructions then re-read them in case you misread. If you still do not understand then ask for clarification from the person who set you the task. Be careful in your wording as saying 'I do not understand' can make you feel incompetent. If you phrase the same statement as 'I just want to check that I've understood this correctly' or 'May I clarify … ' followed by your own explanation of what you think it is asking for, you will sound like you are being diligent, thorough and that you value the test; these are qualities that are sought after in the job market.

If the instructions have been issued verbally, you may also seek clarification through a carefully crafted question. If you do not understand because the instructor or interviewer has a strong accent, has issued the instructions in an unclear manner, or for any other reason, you should verbally summarise the instructions back to check your understanding.

Remember!

If you do not understand something, asking is the only way you can move forward. If you do not have the opportunity to ask, do your best and when you get a chance, explain that you were uncertain and so you went ahead as you thought you should.

What can I learn from a test?

This depends on the test. If it is a personality or aptitude test, you will find out which types of careers you may prefer. Some organisations have games, exercises or quizzes on their websites for prospective employees. This will allow you to find out how well suited to a career you may be.

Other tests may be focused on your level of literacy, numeracy or language skills. These tests will help you establish whether you have the appropriate skill set to complete the jobs you are applying for. As we suggested earlier, you can find these tests online; you could also go to a local adult college and ask to have a diagnostic test.

Do I have the right to the results of any tests I do during selection?

The simple answer is 'yes'. Under the Freedom of Information Act 2000 you are entitled to request access to all information that is held by an organisation about you. This will include emails, any documents that mention your name, and your test results. However, if you ask for your results, they may be happy to issue them to you without you having to go through the formal process of invoking the law. Do keep in mind, though, that the people in the organisation you are dealing with may be extremely busy and so they could take a while to get back to you.

Remember!

Although you will be interested in the results of assessments, do not allow this to hold you up. Keep on with your career plans and activities whilst you wait for copies of your results.

What if I am unhappy with my test results?

The key is to work out which results are leaving you dissatisfied. If it is aptitude tests which are proving most bothersome, you could keep practising online, but you could also go to your local college and ask for help in a specific area. Colleges (both Further Education Colleges and Adult Learning Centres) are excellent at supporting those who need to brush up on specific skills like this.

Careful!

Colleges run by Local Authorities or Government Education Departments will offer help in many areas either for free (especially if you qualify for funding under any government employment-related scheme) or at a modest cost. Universities also offer an impressive range of support services for their students. Beware of private colleges charging substantial fees to provide the same service. If you are working away from your home country be especially vigilant about this – make sure that you have researched the education system before you sign up to anything.

If it is psychometric (personality) tests which trouble you, reflect first on your approach to the tests you have taken. Were you ridiculously nervous, so much so that you answered in a rather random way? Were you so eager to please that you just tried to give what you thought were 'nice' answers about yourself? Do you keep trying to 'beat the test'? If your answer is 'yes' to any of these questions, you can fix the problem the next time you take such a test by simply being truthful and as composed as you can be.

If, on reflection, you do not see the problem as stemming from any of the causes above, but rather that you are not happy with the type of person the tests suggest you are, take this seriously and ponder it from two angles. If it is about your personality ('I want to be outgoing, and I try really hard, but I keep getting test results that tell me I am more introvert than extravert') then remember that this is about the person you are and the genuine preferences you have revealed, rather than the person you want to be. If this is distressing you, talk it through with a friend or mentor.

If it is about the career you are aiming for, make sure that you are clear on how personality preferences can affect career choices. For example, people are often surprised to discover that teaching is a popular choice for introverts, and that they can thrive in that profession. Do not assume that a particular preference somehow disqualifies you for a career you would like – make sure that you have all of the facts. Also remember that these tests reveal preferences, not absolutes, so they should not necessarily be seen as disqualifying you from any job. You also need to balance personality against other forms of career satisfaction. You might not be a great fit for being a chairperson at meetings, but if this is an essential part of a career which you love, you will undertake that task happily in order to get the job.

Remember!

If you choose to see these tests as a way of empowering you, you can use them to take control not just of your next career move, but also of your long-term professional development. If you are inclined to make decisions based on facts and figures rather than people and value judgements, knowing this about yourself will give you the opportunity to consider how important it might be for you to deliberately work in a setting that favours this preference.

Will my psychometric results be likely to change over time?

Yes, to some extent. We have probably all heard of 'nature and nurture', and the idea that some of the ways in which we negotiate our way through life are inherent and part of our genetic coding, and that some are strategies developed over time in response to the people around us and the context in which we live. This can be a pleasing thought – it means that you are not just one person for life, but can develop in different ways as you experience different things.

With this in mind, you will probably want to take a robust view of what these tests can do for you. They can support you in finding the right career for now, and they can help you progress through the selection process if the job is right for you, but they can also reveal something of yourself and so give you a greater sense of purpose.

Careful!

You might be dismayed to find that the variables available on many psychometric tests are quite limited – just two options, perhaps, in an area (such as tending to be either extravert or introvert). Try not to let this make you feel restricted or too pigeonholed. They are uncannily accurate and you are still a unique person even if we do all tend to fall into certain predefined categories.

How important will my results be to a potential employer?

An experienced member of a selection team will know that the results of any test are only one part of the package that a candidate is offering. It is often far more expensive to re-advertise a post and go through the selection process again than it is to train someone up in a particular aspect of a role, so aptitude tests are useful, but not necessarily the final, deciding factor in recruitment. This is an important point to keep in mind, because not doing well at an aptitude test can knock your confidence, but you need to remain positive and focused. If you are still given the chance to interview for the post, you are in with a good chance of being selected.

Psychometric tests show preferences and tendencies – they are not a cast-iron definition of all that you are, and so they should be viewed as indicators rather than constraints. This means that they can give an indication of how you might fit into a team, but it is talking to you that will show whether you truly are the right person for the job. This puts the onus on you to be very clear about what you are happy to do and where you hope to develop. If, for example, you show a preference for taking in information through facts and figures rather than ideas and patterns, but you are going for a role that will require you to work in both of these ways, you can be ready with an example of a situation in which you have worked successfully in a way that works against your natural preference, or you could demonstrate how well you have worked with others who have brought that particular preference to a joint activity.

As with so much else in the selection process, being forewarned and ready to make your case is what will carry you through to success.

What if I am not keen on an aspect of my personality?

Luckily for all of us, we do not have to love every tiny aspect of ourselves in order to have a successful career. Both of us are highly focused – our entire lives are run by lists, documents neatly stowed in plastic wallets and deadlines that will be met, no matter what. However, at times each of us has longed to be less controlled, more open to making decisions by discussion and group dynamics, using less of our judging faculties and more of our perceptive selves. More importantly, we are both in roles that require us to work in a collegiate way from time to time. So, we have deliberately developed strategies in our workplaces that allow us to maximise the benefits of our preferential personality types and overcome the potential weaknesses of our personalities. We do not think that a more perceptive, team approach will ever come naturally to us, but our strategy has given us some great ways to explain to any future employer how we work effectively as part of a creative team.

1.3 My experience

I have not undertaken any work experience, does that matter?

Although work experience is useful on your CV and will help you and others to formulate ideas about which role might suit you, it is not the end of the world if you have little or no work experience. We often find when talking with our students that they have plenty of other useful experiences that prove their employability skills. For example, a mother who had spent ten years out of work caring for her children could confidently state that she had excellent time management skills, proven by the fact that her children were always on time for school and she could successfully manage her course of study during school hours. It is beneficial at this stage to talk with someone from your networks for help in creating a list of experiences that you have had that demonstrate valuable transferable skills.

What counts as experience?

'Experience' could be paid, unpaid, short term, long term, volunteer work, work undertaken as part of a social club. The list goes on. You may have some paid work experience that will not help you get into the career you are aiming for; equally there may have been a volunteer placement that demonstrates the skills required in your desired career. Taking control is partly about deciding which aspect of your experience you want to highlight and which can be left in the background; if you see all of your experience as valuable, you will be in a good position to do this.

Does age matter?

As a younger job seeker, you may be seeing many adverts asking for a certain amount of experience, which you do not necessarily have. This means that you will need to ensure that you are presenting yourself extremely well, including your ability to learn quickly and your eagerness to take on new challenges. Employers will be looking to invest in younger job seekers and to train them up, so you need to appeal to this in your CV and covering letter. You may think that it is only the older generation who need to refresh their offering, such as computer skills, but think again because the younger generation have more trouble with spelling, grammar and writing profes-sionally. You should take the opportunity while you are job searching to do courses that might help you improve your professional writing skills.

If you are an older job seeker with plenty of experience behind you, you should make the most of this. Employers are well aware that younger job seekers are more likely to 'job-hop' and your experience will have given you skills that they need. Therefore, it is vital that you make the most of your experience when applying for jobs. You will also need to prove that you have kept up to date and one very good way of doing this at the outset is to be able to competently and confidently use the computer for filling in online applica-tion forms. If you know that you are not very computer literate, you should do a basic course to improve this skill.

What is an 'experience inventory'?

This is a way to gather together all that you have done, that you would like to foreground in any recruitment situation. Your experience inventory forms the basis of your CV and the examples you will offer at interview (for help in creating this, see Exercise #3).

The exercise we are recommending here is going to take time and reflec-tion, but it is such an important building block to a successful career that we recommend you do it not just once, but twice: we will come back to this idea when we discuss your skills inventory (see page 44).

What are interview 'war stories'?

These are answers you can prepare in advance, ready to respond to standard questions that tend to come up at interview. These might be those that are regularly used ('Why do you think you would suit this job?'; 'Tell me about a time when you had to deal with a work crisis'; 'What is your greatest weakness?') or questions that you can anticipate coming up as a result of your CV ('I notice you carried out an independent research project, can you tell a bit more about that?'; 'You have quite a high level of French – what made you learn a language?').

Your answers to questions like these can be prepared in advance, you can even practise them out loud to make sure that they sound convincing; that way you can control at least some part of the interview process.

Top tip

If you are spending time working up your war stories, make it easier on yourself by thinking of examples that would work to answer several types of question. So, for example, a story about how you placated an irate customer by spending an hour attending to the detail of a complicated query would show how you worked under pressure or how you dealt with a crisis at work. It could also demonstrate a range strengths (meticulous attention to detail, interpersonal skills, problem solving, and analytical ability) and a weakness that is also a strength ('I enjoy the details of a job, and this has sometimes been a problem because I become so engrossed in a problem, but on the other hand it can sometimes be a strength, as in a case recently when we had an irate customer … ').

How can I make my experience look better?

Try to avoid emotional language when you are including experiences on your CV. Your future employer is looking for hard evidence of what you have done and how it makes you suitable for the role. You will have plenty of space on your covering letter/email and ample time at the interview to express how passionate you are about the organisation and the job you have applied for and so your CV must be robust and objective. Use some of the language from the advert if possible as this will help the potential employer to see the connections you have made between their ideal candidate and you.

How can I prove the value of any experience away from paid employment?

Make sure that you fill in as much as you can of column three of your experience inventory – the 'benefits' column. We each of us have different experiences and a potential employer cannot be expected to know the details of how beneficial your experience has been to you or others unless you can give concrete examples backed up by evidence (the benefits) and examples (your war stories will come in handy here). One of us once worked with some-one who had taken a career break for more than twenty years. During that time she claimed, initially, that she had done 'nothing much'. It took some time (and the creation of an experience inventory) for her to reveal that not only had she been president of a society of lace makers for many years, she had also single-handedly produced that society's monthly publication, writ-ing many of the articles herself whilst also collating and editing other members' contributions. It became clear that she had been chronically under-selling herself and it took some time to build her confidence. She now works in the publishing industry as an editor – and loves it.

My experience is a bit scattered. How can I make it more attractive at interview?

The most effective way to approach this is to take control of as much of the interview questioning as you can. Although there will be standard ques-tions of a generic type, such as 'What is your greatest strength?' and similar, there will, naturally, be questions relating to your CV. You will not want to waste precious interview time explaining your CV to someone. It will be clear if there are gaps and/or changes of direction, but you might consider producing a functional CV (we explain this in Step Six, page 113), a document that will highlight your experience and the benefits you can bring to an organisation rather than simply listing your career history. You will still be prepared to talk openly at interview about your career to date, but you will already have gone some way towards showing how this could bring benefits to the organisation.

Do employers care more about qualifications or experience?

This is an interesting question that is often overlooked, and that can be dan-gerous. It might leave you suddenly wondering which is of more importance, and whether you can get a job just with good qualifications even if you do not have the experience, or whether your experience is enough to overcome the fact that you do not have all of the qualifications listed in a person specifica-tion. The answer is simple and reassuring: you will be employed for the totality of what you have to offer. This will include your qualifications, expe-rience, skills, achievements and personal qualities. Focus on the entire package you are offering and judge your chances of success by how well, overall, you fit the profile for the role.

1.4 My qualifications

What are 'my qualifications'?

Your qualifications are any formal qualifications from school, college or university as well as any subsequent courses you have completed in education or the workplace. You will hopefully have certificates or evidence of attendance from any training courses you have undergone.

When an interviewer asks you 'What qualifies you to do this job?' you may talk about more than just your certified qualifications. Your experience may also qualify you to carry out a role. For example, if you have worked for years in an area then your experience will be recognised and you may not need to have the most up-to-date qualification.

It is useful for you to think beyond the courses you have attended. If you have outdated qualifications, it may be that your experience ticks that proverbial or literal box for the interviewer. During interviews, you should explain how your experience qualifies you to do a particular role as the more explicit you can be about this, the easier it is for your potential employer to see how you would benefit the role.

Careful!

You know your qualifications very well, but members of the selection panel might not. Even if your qualifications are in the expert field in which you hope to be employed, some members of the selection team are likely to be from departments in the organisation that are less or differently specialised, or the organisation may have outsourced the process to a general recruitment company. With all of this in the back of your mind, make sure that you make each of your qualifications clear: not just acronyms, but also the full title of each qualification, and if you think there could be any doubt about the title, a brief explanation of just a few words as to what the qualification represents.

What if an advert asks for qualifications that I do not have?

In some instances an advert will ask for qualifications, some of which you may not have. Do not be discouraged: if you are the right person for the role, the organisation may want to take you on with the proviso that you will start working towards those qualifications. If you notice that most of the jobs you want to apply for demand a certain qualification that you do not have, it is worth gaining this as soon as possible. The impact of signing up to a course is huge as it demonstrates to your prospective employers that you are committed to the job role you are chasing and that you are willing to pay and/or give up time to do this.

> **Remember!**
>
> An advertisement is outlining the perfect candidate for a role; this does not mean that the employer will get a perfect candidate walking through the door. With this in mind, you should apply for the role even if you do not satisfy every desirable criterion. Do not forget to check to see if you have qualities and skills that would benefit the role even if they are not listed in the advert. Do your research, be honest with yourself, and then stride forward with confidence.

In what order should my qualifications be presented on my CV?

Start with your most recent qualifications and work back through your older qualifications. Unless an advert specifically asks for English, mathematics or ICT skills, just put the number of GCSE-level qualifications you have followed by 'including English, mathematics and ICT'. If the advert asks for a certain level of English or mathematics then you will need to put the grade in brackets next to the subject. Generally speaking, the more recent the qualification, the more detail you are likely to give.

> **Careful!**
>
> We know that it can be incredibly hard to leave off your CV qualifications of which you are justifiably proud, but you need to accentuate what you are offering in this particular situation and for this particular job. An irrelevant qualification is simply taking up space that could be used to sell yourself more effectively. If space allows and you believe that a qualification, whilst not directly relevant, says something important about you and your qualities, you could include it under an 'Additional Information' section towards the end of your CV, as an interesting talking point at interview.

What if I have failed an exam?

This is a tricky question to answer. As a general rule, we would say that there is no need to include any qualifications that you have failed. If you are resitting an exam to be able to achieve a certain qualification then you simply need to state 'working towards [insert the name of the qualification] and due to complete in [date you expect to achieve it]'.

However, if the course that you were on is required to be able to undertake a job role for which you are applying, then you will want to be able to tell your potential employer that you have done some work towards achieving the qualification. In these circumstances it would make sense to include 'Course undertaken in … ' to make it clear that you have studied on the course even though you did not achieve exam success. If you have failed due to unavoidable circumstances such as ill health, a bereavement, or other similar reasons, you may choose to discuss this at interview but do not put it on your CV.

What if I have dropped out of a course?

If you feel that what you have learnt from the course is valuable in your application then do mention it on your CV as 'course undertaken in … ' or, if you dropped out quite a way from the end of the course, 'course commenced in … ', but be ready for questions about this. Keep in mind that your future employer may see this as a negative thing unless you have an extremely good reason why it happened. If you are asked, simply explain why you dropped out of a course and state what you are currently doing, or planning to do, to rectify the situation.

What if I have not completed a course yet?

This is an excellent opportunity for you to show your prospective employers that you are still actively developing your skills. It also gives them a good idea of how you will benefit their organisation in the future. You may start on a lower salary due to still being in education or training but you will have a foothold in the organisation and when you have completed the relevant course then your salary should go up.

You have worked hard to get onto the course, you are still working diligently to complete it and you should be proud of what you are doing to improve your employability, so talk about it! Remember that your CV is a chance for you to show off your skills and the only aim of your CV is to get you to an interview where you can really wow them.

Top tip

This is an easy way to show dedication to a potential employer. If the job description or person specification makes it obvious that conversational Spanish would be an advantage, sign up to a course straightaway. That way, you can mention it on your CV even before you actually begin the course. If conversational Spanish is not really your thing, you can always abandon the idea if the job does not come through for you.

What if I gained my qualifications in a different country from where I want to work?

NARIC is a useful organisation that you can access online, which compares overseas qualifications to UK qualifications. This will allow you to state that you have an overseas qualification that equates to, for example, an A Level grade B in the subject (www.naric.org.uk is the website you can go to for this service).

What if I do not have any evidence of my qualifications because I lost them or I have not yet received my certificate?

If you have lost your certificates, see if you can get hold of them again by going back to the institution with which you qualified. They will probably charge you for a new certificate as most awarding organisations charge a fee to reissue these. If you are unable to do this because the organisation has shut down, you can go directly to the awarding body and request your certificate again. If your certificate is very old, you may find that a new certificate is hard to get but that a record of your successful completion is available. Again, some educational establishments are able to give you a record to prove that you completed a course, even if you are struggling to get hold of a new certificate.

This is also useful if you have yet to receive your certificate for a recently completed course. Start off by contacting the institution where you qualified; ask when your certificate is likely to come through and if there is going to be a significant wait, then ask if they would write a letter to prove that you have passed your course. Most organisations will be able to verify this statement by using a company stamp or headed paper.

Top tip

You will not normally be asked to send accompanying certificates with your CV or application form, so include all of the relevant qualifications in those documents even if you are not sure you can produce a certificate. If a qualification is very old, of course, you must ask yourself first whether it is still relevant. If it is, put it on there and only try to get hold of a copy certificate if you are specifically asked to do this by the potential employer.

What if I have done some training but there is no certificate?

Training that you have undertaken that is not certified will still count towards the overall package that you are offering any organisation. For educational qualifications and many national professional qualifications you would expect to be given a certificate, but if you undertook a course in team-building, for example, you might have it on your record as an employee but have no independent verification. This need not be a problem. You list the course under 'Professional Development' on your CV and on application forms. You believe that it will help sell you, so you will give brief details of what the course entailed and you can talk about it at interview. The fact that there is no certificate becomes irrelevant.

If you are not sure what counts as 'education' and what counts as 'professional development', think of it this way: an educational course is undertaken at a school, college, university or other educational establishment and is nationally certified; a professional development course might take place anywhere and may or may not be certified.

What is an 'in-house' qualification?

An in-house qualification is given for any training that is provided by your employer normally in your place of work. The trainer might be an independent professional, but the training takes place as part of your work and, usually, in your normal working hours. The training will be directly relevant to your job role within the organisation. You would not always receive a certificate for this type of training, but you should still include it both on your CV and application forms.

Do not be too tough on yourself here. If you received a half-day induction course when you first started to work in a restaurant, that is in-house training in customer care, or Health and Safety awareness, or whatever was the main topic of the training. Avoid telling yourself that it was not 'proper training'; if you benefited from the session, were able to put it into practice in your workplace and would be happy to discuss it at interview, it goes on your CV, to distinguish you from other candidates who might not have undertaken any training at all.

How much professional development should go on my CV?

When you build your 'master CV', as we advise you to do in Step Six (see page 115), you will include all of your educational qualifications alongside all of your training and professional development activities. If you are thorough you will probably be surprised at how much you have done, and it is likely that there will be too much material to fit onto your two-page CV, but having it all on the master CV allows you to focus on targeting each opportunity, making your sales pitch with the most relevant and attractive material.

You might find some grey areas when you come to list all of your educational qualifications, training and professional development activities, and this can be a good thing. For example, an introductory course in web design that you undertook whilst at college could be seen as education, but then the certificate for it might be an NVQ (a National Vocational Qualification), which might class it as training; on the other hand, it is a talent you developed as part of your employability and so it could be seen as professional development. When it comes to filling out an application form we would urge you always to try to make a convincing case in each space you are offered, so you can use this sort of activity to fill out an otherwise empty or sparse space.

Should I ask about additional qualification opportunities at interview?

Yes, but gently. When you are asked if you have any questions (usually towards the end of an interview), asking about personal and professional development opportunities is a great way to show that you are flexible, keen to learn and happy to work hard. However, reeling off a list of training and qualifications that you would like the employer to pay for might sound a bit grasping and may also leave the interviewer wondering if you will actually have time to do the job.

The training opportunities you bring up should therefore usually be restricted to four circumstances:

1. Any area of the person specification where you know you are not fully up to strength.
2. Any aspect of the job description that you feel less confident about but where you can see an opening for some training.
3. Any qualification that you have and that is needed for the job but that will lapse soon – this shows how well qualified you are already, and how committed you are to keeping your qualifications up to date.
4. Any training they have mentioned. Picking up on this shows that you are listening carefully to what is on offer and are happy to engage fully with both the role and your own development.

You are asking about development opportunities so as to look keen – and because you would genuinely like to receive more training – not so as to put the employer on the spot. Ask the question, note the answer, look pleased with what you are told and move on. You can find out more about the details at a later stage in the selection process, particularly if you are choosing between two competing offers.

1.5 My qualities

What are qualities?

Qualities are the aspects of your personality that make you, you. You might have plenty of skills, but what makes you excel at these are your qualities.

Learning how to set up a webpage is acquiring a skill, but having the patience to create webpages is the quality that allows you to use that skill. That is why qualities are so important to employers: having a customer care representative with no patience, or a salesperson with no drive, or a counsellor with little empathy, is dooming an organisation to failure. You might have heard of career competencies and these are relevant here – being able to do something well by bringing together a skill and a quality is a competency.

As you progress through your career plans, you will find that being able to articulate and examine your qualities is going to become important to you, too. Throughout our lives we often take on roles and responsibilities because we have a certain qualification, or have acquired a particular skill, but now you have the chance to identify your most important qualities and find a career not only in which you can excel but also feel comfortable. As with much else we will be discussing with you in this guide, this is about taking control.

One of us spent several years chairing meetings for various groups at work. She had assumed that she would be the person to take on this role because she has always been an organised person. She was fine with getting the papers to everyone on time, arranging the agenda and booking rooms for meetings, but it took her a surprisingly long time to work out that she has very little patience in group situations. She was always keen to have her say and to get to the end of each meeting on time but she was not an effective chairperson; it came as a relief to both her and her colleagues when she realised her error and passed the chairing over to a person far better temperamentally suited to the role!

What do employers want?

Employers want the right person for the job. This 'right person' may not have all of the qualifications or experience that is mentioned on the job advert; this is why employers will often use aptitude or psychometric tests to establish which candidates will 'fit in'. In the first instance, your CV should outline your qualities to get you to an interview; once in the interview, you will need to be able to explain your qualities in an articulate manner, which is something that you should practise. You have already taken the first step to being a successful applicant for the role you want because you have bought this book, which tells us that you are committed to presenting yourself effectively. By undertaking the exercises suggested in this book and taking the time to really understand what you want and how to get it, you are more likely not just to get interviews, but also to excel at them (see Exercise #4 to begin to understand what your future employer is looking for).

How do I highlight my qualities?

Your qualities should always be backed up by examples of when they have been demonstrated. It is very easy to state on an application form or in an interview that you cope well under pressure, but by giving evidence of this through examples you will be proving those qualities. You may get the opportunity to demonstrate some of your qualities through a practical element in an interview, such as being a 'good listener'.

This is the beginning of you being able to come up with 'war stories' (see page 20) at interview (more about this in Step One), namely concrete examples that prove what you are claiming about yourself. It is far more convincing to a potential employer if, rather than just claiming that you are a good team player, you are able to recount an incident where you had to bring a team together, or where you achieved success as part of a team.

Must I prove my qualities?

You do need to prove your qualities because you want to make it as easy as possible for others to understand how you will fit into a role, as they might be seeing many applicants during the recruitment process and so they are not going to spend a great deal of time trying to draw out your qualities and the evidence that they truly exist.

People who know you well can be hugely valuable here. You know a version of yourself, of course, but do you really know all about yourself? By asking others how they see you, especially close family, friends and colleagues, you might be surprised at how you are perceived. It could be that you never thought of yourself as particularly calm in a crisis, but this is how others view you. You might not feel that they are always accurate in their analysis – maybe you have been putting on a façade for years – but they will give you food for thought.

What are my most important career qualities?

Once you have decided to go into a career, you should look at the qualities sought for in job adverts. You could also talk to those already in the career area to find out what they think are the qualities most valuable to that field. You may also find that the websites of your target organisations have more information about the qualities that they value and this research will benefit you when you are targeting your CV, covering letter and interview.

> **Careful!**
>
> Rather than looking at the totality of your many qualities, here we are talking only about what we would term 'career qualities' – those qualities that you would be happy to utilise on a daily basis as part of making a living. There might be other qualities that are important to you that you would prefer not to use at work each day.

Are there qualities I should ignore?

If you are a generous friend or a thrill-seeking adventurer, you may decide that these qualities are not particularly attractive or useful to your future employer. Do your research carefully so that you know that you are highlighting the qualities that will most appeal to the organisation you are targeting.

What about my achievements?

Your achievements are important and you should mention them on your CV and, if the opportunity arises, at interview. Be slightly selective with your achievements; although you may be very pleased that you won a role-playing competition, this may have no relevance to the job you wish to undertake. However, achievements such as securing funding for a project may well be of interest to the employer who is searching for a fundraiser or someone who can produce effective business cases.

1.6 My motivation

How much does my motivation matter?

Your motivation matters a great deal. Starting a new career is rarely easy and will take much effort and energy on your part, however great your support network is. If you are not feeling motivated, then you are less likely to achieve your goals. Our students find it useful fairly early on in their journey to identify what motivates them; it is also important to be able to recognise what demotivates them. Take some time to think about what is motivating you to start or change the career path you have selected. Is it prospective earnings or similar benefits? Is it to be able to have more free time? Is it to use a skill you feel passionate about? Is it to join friends? If you have multiple reasons to search for a new career this may be more helpful to you as time goes on, as sometimes the original reason for doing something can fade away.

By recognising what demotivates you, you can avoid anything that might prevent you from being successful in your acquisition of a new career.

A useful website that can help you find out what motivates you is https://psychologies.co.uk/tests/what-motivates-you.html

---

Remember!

This is a hugely important point on your road to success. You need to be honest with yourself and think about what really motivates you rather than what you feel should motivate you, or what friends and family tell you might inspire or demotivate you. Be blunt here: if money is your key motivation, for example, be clear with yourself so that you know that you might have to be prepared to miss out on other things in order to chase that money. Your friends and family might admire you more if you were to say that 'making a difference' is your key motivator, but if making a difference involves giving up on several other key motivating features of a career, you are unlikely to be content.

What might motivate me?

There are two types of motivation: intrinsic (coming from you) and extrinsic (coming from outside of you). In an ideal world you would have a little bit of both pushing you forward. Intrinsic motivation, although more temperamental, is the stronger type of motivation as it comes from your own desire to take action and so will help you to persevere and enjoy the challenges. This motivation may come from your passion for a subject, your desire to progress or learn, or your predicted sense of pride when you succeed.

Extrinsic motivation can still be a powerful thing and usually derives from the expectation of a salary increase, a promotion or another external reward. Start to think about your own motivation by completing Exercise #5 at the back of this book.

Remember!

By remembering what motivated you in the first place, you can find renewed energy and enthusiasm to overcome barriers and face challenges to your success. Smiling at your list of motivators sets off a series of physiological triggers that tell your brain you are happy and this will relax you, which makes any challenges seem possible to overcome.

How about demotivation, in my career choice and my career action plan?

The factors offered in the section above all relate to what might motivate or demotivate you in your career, but it is also likely that, at some stage, you will begin to feel demotivated in the job-hunting process itself. It is easy to feel that you are not making much progress, or that you are never going to find the best career for you. If this happens to you, take action immediately – feeling demotivated in what you are trying to do can really set you back unless you tackle it straightaway.

We often become demotivated when barriers seem insurmountable and our energy is low. Take some time away from the task and do something easy and relaxing. This will give your brain and body time to recover and, while you are doing that, a small part of your brain will be untangling the knot of the problem you put to one side. Before you return to the challenge, make sure that you have eaten something (not too heavy or you might get drowsy), drunk plenty (this has been proven to improve concentration and brain power), and that you go back in a positive frame of mind.

A second option is to talk with somebody about the issue you have encountered, even if that is simply that you are tired of working away at the task. A problem shared is almost always a problem halved and educational institutions have support services on hand to help at moments like this.

Remember!

A little tip from us is that you should select a friend or colleague who will listen patiently and tell you how wonderful you are as you will certainly feel more capable after a pep talk!

How does self-motivation match to a career?

Although we have been considering with you the factors that might motivate you to choose one career over another, there is also the importance of self-motivation, that intrinsic sense of simply wanting to get the job done. Some careers will require you to be highly self-motivated, particularly those in which you will be doing much of the work alone. If you know that you struggle to self-motivate, these careers will feel like a colossal struggle and exhaust you. Some careers incorporate extrinsic motivators such as deadlines, pay rises, development opportunities and promotions. If you are not keen about constantly working towards the next prescribed step, you will find these careers to be stressful and limited.

This is not about whether you are a 'good worker' or 'work-shy', it is just that some of us prefer clearly defined, externally produced goals, whilst others of us are happy to work away regardless of the goals, or are prepared to make our own goals to keep us motivated. Finding out which sort of person you are will play a large part in securing a role that will make you happy and – importantly – lead to career success.

How do values fit into this?

In the context of your career journey, your values are the qualities that you appreciate. For example, you may appreciate honesty, diligence, determination, and/or clarity of purpose. You should consider what your values are when thinking about what motivates you as you can use these as tools to help you go forward. For example, you may value a close family life and so use this to motivate you towards a well-paid career that can help you afford a comfortable home life.

Remember!

Values are not just about you – they are also about how you see the world. Each organisation will have values, whether they are explicitly stated or not, and so you will want to examine these to make sure that they fit in with your values and how you see your place in life. We were both drawn to work principally in education because we both approve of the values of that world, the sense of giving to others, sharing great ideas and helping people to develop.

Whose motivations matter most?

Your own motivations matter most. You should know why are you are doing something as this reasoning will help you target your approach and seek out fulfilling employment.

You may have people in your life who try to transfer their own motivations onto you. However, we recommend that you are honest with yourself – ultimately this will make you happier in your career.

Careful!

This is the right stage in your career journey to be thinking about your motivation and your values, but later on you will have to consider also the motivation and values of an employer. An interview in which you simply recite a set of values and motivators, and in which you list what you think you can get from the job, is unlikely to be successful. Instead you are looking for a good fit between what motivates you and what is motivating your potential employer in looking to employ someone.

1.7 Knowing my worth

What is my education worth?

Your education is worth a great deal when it comes to applying for a job. It will show the skills you already have, and those subjects for which you have an aptitude, and it will allow potential employers to ascertain whether you will be able to fulfil a role within their organisation.

Top tip

Not everyone will necessarily understand why aspects of their education are relevant to a job – remember that the person interviewing you may have had a very different education. Rather than just listing courses on your CV, make an effort to highlight any parts of a course that could be of interest or benefit to an employer.

What are my skills worth?

As with your education, your skills are a valuable asset. You may not have a certificate to evidence all of your skills but your references should support your claim to those skills. Your professional skills will sometimes be considered more important than your education, and certainly in practical roles those skills could be held in higher esteem than your education.

Top tip

When you are offering your skills to an organisation, in a CV, email or application form, try to be as specific as you can. 'IT skills' can mean anything; 'Excellent IT skills' is a little better, but 'Working knowledge of Excel and a wealth of experience in Client Management Systems' is a far more enticing offer.

What are my values worth?

Some organisations will be searching for specific values in candidates and so it is useful to research the organisation in some detail. Although important, these are not as significant in getting you that dream job as your education, skills and experience.

Remember that, until you get as far as an interview, this is not a conversation. Your potential employer cannot ask you to explain yourself more fully, or suggest that you elaborate. For this reason, tread lightly with your values. They will match the organisation's values or requirements (that is why you are applying for the role), but if you word it carelessly you could obscure your true meaning. Values are delicate things, and 'making a difference in the wider world' could be off-putting if you are asking to fill a role where profit, not social welfare, is the key driver.

What is my experience worth?

Experience is vital to a good application, but luckily we all have some experience. As mentioned earlier, if you do not have an abundance of work-related experience, draw on other experiences you have had that prove you have desirable skills and knowledge for the workplace.

People are sometime afraid that 'plenty of experience' could be read as 'a bit too old for this job', but let us reassure you that no sensible employer would turn down the chance to gain relevant and useful experience. It is also worth noting that 24 year-olds have complained to us about ageism in the workplace, as well as 54 year-olds. Having said that, if you have had a chequered career with several diversions and digressions, you might want to consider a functional CV rather than the standard chronological CV, so that you can really highlight what you are offering. There is more on this in Step Six of this guide (particularly on page 113).

What are my connections worth?

According to some research, 90% of your success rate into your new career could be all down to the connections that you have used effectively. You may feel awkward drawing on the connections you have but we hope that the numbers will persuade you that a few minutes spent asking someone to help you could save you both time and unnecessary effort.

You do not have to be what society might consider 'well-connected' in order to have useful connections. We are not thinking here about social connections or class; we are talking about remembering to make the most of the connections you have from previous jobs, or tutors/mentors who have helped you, or family and friends who can provide you with useful information, even if not an introduction.

How much salary am I worth?

When trying to work out how much salary you could expect, you should look at the salaries of the types of jobs you wish to secure. If you have fewer qualifications or less experience than those jobs tend to require, you will likely start on a lower salary. Salaries vary across the country and in cities you can expect to be paid more due to the higher cost of living.

Even if you have a good idea of what you think your salary should be, it can be tricky if you are asked this question at interview. In Step Seven (see page 126) we will guide you through this potential interview minefield. (You may want to use the website www.reed.co.uk/average-salary or similar to gain an approximate idea of the salary you could expect.)

Should I accept a job role that is not quite what I want?

At times you might feel disillusioned and want to accept whatever offer you get. We urge you to think very carefully before you agree to take on a role that is not what you were seeking. Doing so can lead to disasters such as leaving within weeks of starting (which will be demoralising and upsetting) or taking a series of 'not quite' jobs in a row, which could leave you with a career history that suggests a lack of commitment.

Despite these possible pitfalls, it can be a positive move forward in your career to accept a position that is paid at a lower salary or is not quite what you were searching for if it is in an organisation that you were hoping to work for; you could use this as another opportunity to continue on the path to your dream career.

If you decide to take a second choice job on in order to earn money while you continue to search for a way into your preferred career, that might be seen as a reasonable move, but make sure that you plan your timing so as to commit to that search – time has a way of flying past while we are busy earning a living.

Remember!

The networks that you build up within an organisation could help you into the job role that you covet. Many job opportunities surface on the grapevine (or the intranet) of companies before they are publicly advertised and so you will hear about them first. Hearing about these jobs as they become available will give you time to ask colleagues for their help in constructing a perfect application, as you can find out exactly what they are looking for and target your application and interview very precisely.

1.8 Managing the process

This part of your career journey takes patience, honesty and sheer determination. At times you will be tempted to skip through part of the process ('Do I really have time to work up a full experience inventory [see page 149], when I just want to get on with things?', you might ask yourself). At other points you may feel awkward (these exercises require honesty, both from other people and with yourself.) Some of it is tedious (who knew it could be so boring to think about yourself and your motivation for hours?!) and you will have to persevere, aware that it is vital that you get this right. The dangers of getting it wrong are, by now, all too obvious. You could find yourself in the wrong job for you, working behind a façade of the person you said you were rather than who you really are, and finding very little career satisfaction. It might take time and effort to complete Step One on your path to success, but it is preferable to the alternative of having to start all over again in a year's time when you realise you are not happy. If you grit your teeth and keep going now, you are radically improving your chances of real success.

Further reading

As part of managing the process, you may find it useful to do further research using these recommended websites:

1.2 My personality and preferences

Personality tests:

www.myersbriggs.org – The Myers & Briggs Foundation allows you the opportunity to find out more about your personality and it is commonly used across both business and education.

www.humanmetrics.com/cgi-win/jtypes2.asp – This is a Jung typology test that is free to do and will help you understand what your personality type is.

www.personalitypathways.com/type_inventory.html – This website gives you some more information about how to understand and use your personality type as identified by the Myers-Briggs test.

http://personality-testing.info/tests/RIASEC.php – This is a test often used by careers advisors to help you work out which career path may suit you best.

www.businessballs.com/johariwindowmodel.htm – This website explains what the Johari window is and how it helps you improve your self-awareness and your communication within a team.

www.humanresourcefulness.net/CypressCollege/docs/HUSR224/Johari_Window_Questionnaire-package.pdf – This is a Johari window questionnaire to explore more about yourself in relation to a team you might be working in or planning to work in.

How you fit into a team:

www.belbin.com/rte.asp – This test establishes how you fit into a team.

Example of an aptitude test:

www.gov.uk/civil-service-fast-stream-how-to-apply – This website shows you how to apply for various civil service careers and also gives you the opportunity to practise some of the aptitude tests.

1.3 My experience

Work experience inventory template:

http://hrweb.berkeley.edu/files/attachments/Work-Experience-Inventory.pdf – This is a useful worksheet for you to complete to focus on the types of experiences that you have had, which will be beneficial to you during the application process.

1.4 My qualifications

Converting foreign qualifications to UK system:

www.naric.org.uk – If you have achieved qualifications outside of the UK and would like to know what they are equivalent to in the UK system, use this website to convert them.

What qualification levels mean:

www.gov.uk/what-different-qualification-levels-mean/overview – This is a government website that explains different UK qualifications.
https://nationalcareersservice.direct.gov.uk/advice/courses/Pages/QualificationsTable. aspx – This website explains both current and historic qualifications and how they fit into the current Qualifications and Credit Framework in the UK.

1.5 My qualities

Skills that employers are looking for:

www.kent.ac.uk/careers/sk/top-ten-skills.htm – This website has plenty of useful information for students entering the career market. This particular page lists the top skills looked for by employers.

1.6 My motivation

Motivation quiz:

https://psychologies.co.uk/tests/what-motivates-you.html – This short quiz will tell you what usually drives you and gives you some brief advice about how to ensure that you stay motivated.

Article about motivation:

www.bps.org.uk/news/motivation-more-important-intelligence — This is an interesting article about how important motivation is.

1.7 Knowing my worth

Knowing what salary you can command:

www.reed.co.uk/average-salary — This job site offers you some information about the sort of salary you can expect depending on your field of work. It also gives you information about how many vacancies there are in each job type in the UK, although this is not a precise figure.

Step Two: Making your skills work for you

Read this section now if:

- You are unsure what skills are.
- You do not know what skills you have.
- You would like to gain more skills but do not know where to start.
- You do not know how to sell your skills effectively.
- You are uncertain about how to handle it if you do not have the skills that a prospective employer wants.

2.1 Introduction: why does it matter?

It is simple, really. If you do not know what skills you have, you cannot expect a prospective employer to be able to recognise these. Equally, if you do not know what skills your future employer wants, you will struggle to tailor your CV and interview to match these.

2.2 My skills base

What is a skill?

A skill is defined in *The Concise Oxford Dictionary* as 'expertness, practised ability, facility in doing something, dexterity, tact'. Maybe you are still wondering about what skills you should be looking for in yourself. If this is the case then ask yourself this: 'What am I good at doing?' Once you know what you are good at doing, you can start weeding out the skills that are not relevant to work, such as 'making a very good tissue paper fairy for the children' or 'playing computer games' (unless you are going into a craft job or wanting to test new computer games).

Careful!

We are asking you here to define and promote the skills you have, rather than just things you have done. That is, you need to identify what you are *good* at doing. We are all capable of cleaning a bathroom, for example, but would you say it is just something you have to do, or are you so good at it that you would class it as a skill to promote to an employer?

How does it differ from my experience?

Your experience should demonstrate that you have used a skill or set of skills effectively.

Remember!

A 'skill' is something that you can do; 'experience' is something that you have been through. Your experience should demonstrate the skills that you claim to have.

How recently should I have used a skill?

The more recently, the better, as this shows that you have up-to-date skills and that you are not out of practice with them. However, if you have not used a skill for a number of years, you may need to retrain or do a refresher course. Some skills are transferable, such as task management, and so you may not have used these in the workplace in years but you could have evidence of using them in your personal life.

Remember!

Although we would urge you to foreground skills that are current, if a skill is vital to a role and is something that you never really lose (such as telephone work), put it on your CV even if the example you offer to prove that skill is from many years ago.

When you itemise skills on your CV in this way you are not going to be offering dates, so the selection team will not know immediately that this is a skill you acquired some time ago.

How do I pull the skills out of a situation?

Reflection is important to find out more about yourself in preparation for applying for a new career opportunity. Think objectively about the skills you have used in a situation and consider if these are likely to be useful for the role you are targeting. Sometimes we can salvage useful skills from bad situations. For example, if your post has been made redundant, the way in which you handled it could prove that you cope with stress and pressure by remaining calm; you may have also demonstrated self-motivation and initiative by going on training courses before you left your position. You might think that these are your personal qualities, and they are, but your skills in putting them into play could be making a database of career contacts or developing new skills on the courses you attended. (Complete Exercise #6 at the back of the book to start compiling a list of your skills.)

How do I pull the skills out of a qualification?

Think about the skills you used to complete the qualification. For example, your degree or college course demanded that you plan, write and review lengthy essays. The skills that this demonstrates are excellent planning skills, namely the ability to write in formal English and useful reflective skills to improve on your own work.

Remember!

By going back to the course description, you could find a list or details about what the course was going to 'give you'. These are sometimes called the learning outcomes, and could provide a useful starting point in your skills analysis.

Are there any skills that I should ignore?

Yes. Any skills that are not relevant to the position for which you are applying, you can safely ignore for the time being. If they become pertinent at a later stage then you can bring them out. For example, you may not include these on your CV because you do not believe them to be relevant to the job; however, during your interview, if you see an opportunity to raise the fact that you have an additional skill, you will naturally do so.

Remember!

People sometimes assume that, just because you are good at something, you must be naturally talented in that area and must also enjoy using that skill. One of us once spent a laborious summer learning how to make ploughman's lunches in a busy pub. It turned out that she is an excellent ploughman's lunch maker – but she never wants to see one again, for the rest of her life.

2.3 Identifying my skills

What if I have no skills?

We can say with 100% certainty that you do have skills and have just not identified them yet.

What is a skills inventory?

This is the same in principle as the experience inventory we worked through with you in Step One (see page 20 and Exercise #3 at the back of the book). It is a way of identifying and recording all of your relevant skills – that is, those skills that you are best at and would like to use in the future. So, this is a time to itemise both your skills and the evidence to prove you have these, but it is also time to abandon any mention of skills that you no longer wish to use.

A skills inventory, like its experience counterpart, is a wide-ranging document that encompasses all of the skills you are happy to offer an organisation. At this stage, try not to have a particular career area or job role in mind; just list your skills so that you have the fullest possible inventory, and then later we will help you narrow these down as you focus on a role.

How do I create my skills inventory?

This is going to take time, but it will be worth it when you can look at a huge list of skills and realise that you will be a valuable asset to an organisation, so go to Exercise #7 to get started on creating your skills inventory.

Who can help me?

It would be ideal if you could find at least three people to help you in this task and then take a three-step approach as detailed below.

Success checklist

✓ Ask a supporter to talk you through your situations and the skills involved and then ask that person to jot these down or type them into your table as you go. It is surprising to find how many more skills you can pull out from a situation if someone is prompting you.

✓ Once you have made an initial list, ask someone to talk you through each of the situations you have used, making sure that you have pulled out all possible skills and examples of benefits.

✓ When you are fairly sure that you have captured everything you need for now (knowing that you will probably return to this again in the future to add to it), ask a third supporter to have a final peruse of the document. This person has two goals: to check that you have not left out any situations or skills, and to help you decide which of your examples of benefits is the most impressive or most useful to you in terms of a 'multi-purpose war story' at interview.

Must I have a certificate/qualification to prove my skills?

No – some of your skills will be certificated because you took a course in them, but others will simply be proved by a convincing example.

What if I have too many skills?

You will have – we all do. Once you have worked up a skills inventory (see page 44) you will probably be astounded at the range of skills you possess. That is why we know that the last stage of the exercises above – grouping your skills and highlighting the best examples of benefits – is so vital. That way you have a manageable amount of material to make a convincing sales pitch for yourself.

What if I am uncertain about a skill?

Do nothing until you are sure that you will need to use this skill regularly in the position you are targeting. Then ask yourself why you are uncertain – is it because you do not like using the skill, or because you are not especially adept at it? If the former, you will need to be wary – make sure that the skill does not make up a large proportion of the requirements of the job before you go ahead. As we have said already, you need to take control and move on from those skills that you find least rewarding.

2.4 Boosting my skills

Which skills should I focus on boosting?

It makes sense to be as analytical as possible here, because you will not want to spend time brushing up on a skill that you do not especially need, or where you are already able to display more than enough competence. (To start focusing on which of your skills need boosting, complete Exercise #8 at the back of the book.)

> **Careful!**
>
> In those areas where there is a gap between your skill level and the role requirements, take a moment to consider. Do not rush off and sign up for a training course instantly! If there is a huge gap this might give you cause for concern, but moderate gaps are to be expected and you may well be able to make up for a skills gap with other assets you have that you can highlight in your interview, or it might be that the employer is already intending to offer training in a skill area to the successful candidate.

How can I gain more skills quickly?

Take opportunities that arise to develop old skills and gain new skills. These opportunities could come in the form of formal training courses or volunteer placements. You might be wary of volunteering as it is unpaid but we recommend that you see it as an opportunity to develop skills. Use a spiderweb chart to target your search for upskilling opportunities. This will ensure that you find the process rewarding and beneficial in your search for a job (www.kent.ac.uk/careers/sk/skillsmenu.htm is a useful website for looking at all of your skills and giving you information about how to boost them; it is from Kent University and so focuses on students but is still helpful to others).

Taking a course, working in the voluntary sector or finding other opportunities to boost your skills base will offer you more than just additional selling points on your CV. It will also keep your motivation and energy levels high and help keep you focused on the career goal ahead of you – it is a win–win situation.

What skills development opportunities should I look out for?

You should look out for training courses run at your place of work or study, alongside e-learning courses, workshops and courses run by your local colleges, and volunteer placements. You will find that some courses are funded for adults and so it is worthwhile checking with your local college to find out what is available as it might not be as expensive as you think.

It is sometimes worth going for a slightly different role within an organisation you are targeting, one that more closely matches your current skills base, as there may be an opportunity to change roles at a later date and you will have had a chance to prove and develop your skills. As we mentioned earlier, having a connection to an organisation is of huge benefit when going for a job.

Learning a new language is a very good use of your time and money as the careers marketplace has become global. Many companies have contacts across the world and to have even a basic understanding of another language will help you build a rapport with these colleagues and clients.

2.5 Selling my skills

How will my skills help my CV profile?

Your skills are an essential part of your CV as this is the section that really helps your prospective employer to appreciate the benefits of employing you. Your CV is a chance to show off your skills, experience, qualities and qualifications. At this point, modesty is not a virtue but a hindrance to successfully selling yourself. Make sure that you give examples of when you have used your skills and in your interview refer to those skills when explaining how well-suited you are for the role.

> **Top tip**
>
> If you list your skills near the beginning of your CV, with brief evidence to prove that you actually have the skill (and perhaps the personal quality to excel in that skill), any potential employer will be impressed by your sales pitch even before perusing the detail that comes later on the CV.

How can social media help my skills base?

At the most practical, day-to-day level, most regular social media users are being given an opportunity to market themselves effectively, and that means highlighting your skills base in any situation where you are aware that an employer might be browsing. We talk in Step Five about cleaning up your personal brand on social media (see page 101), but this is a chance to showcase your skills if you sign up to the social media platforms (such as LinkedIn™) that specialise in professional networking.

However, social media can do more than just promote skills you already have, they are also helping you develop skills in networking, articulating your ideas and showing an ability to develop your understanding of particular issues in society. These are all useful skills and your social media activity can form the basis of war stories (see page 20) at interview that your interviewer is likely to relate to easily.

> **Remember!**
>
> LinkedIn complements and does not mirror your CV and so your profile should be more personal and engaging.

How can I prove myself online?

We are living in a time when our online presence can have a huge impact upon achieving a good career for ourselves. If you are applying for a role in management and your potential employers search for you online, they will not be impressed if all they can find is a selection of photos on Facebook or other social media showing you drunk or behaving in an irresponsible way. You should do an online search of yourself and see what comes up. Once you know what is already out there, you can either remove or add information to boost your professional online profile. We mention this here, but in Step Five (see page 99) we will go into more detail with you about how to create an effective 'personal brand' both in person and online.

> **Remember!**
>
> An organisation that uses the internet and professional networking or social media sites is more likely to search for you online than those organisations that have a limited online presence. The former types of organisations will be more impressed and put more stock in your professional online presence than the latter.

How assertive should I be in selling my skills?

You should be assertive as this is your opportunity to show off your skills to potential employers. Remember that there is a difference between being assertive and being arrogant or aggressive. We recommend that you remain positive in the language you use when talking about your skills and always tie this back into the role you are applying for if possible. For example, 'I have excellent time management skills as proven when I was doing two jobs and an evening course and I never missed a deadline. I believe that this would benefit me in this new job role as I understand that there will be time pressures and deadlines to which I will need to work.'

How can my skills help me in an interview?

Not only should you refer to your skills and the benefits of these to the organisation in your interview, you should also demonstrate these during the interview. Let us show you how …

Action	Skill demonstrated
Arrive early	Time keeping
Smile at the interviewer(s) and shake their hand	Confident with good communication skills
Answering questions clearly and making eye contact with the interviewer(s)	Excellent communication skills and active listening skills
Using their names and referring to the research you have done about the organisation	Well-prepared with useful research skills A good memory and understanding of the organisation

What if I do not have all of the skills they want?

As mentioned earlier, sometimes you will not have all of the skills, qualifications or experience that an organisation wants. However, do not be discouraged. During the interview focus mainly on the skills that you do have, the skills they have not asked for but that you think will be useful to the role, and then explain that you are in the process of developing the skills you do not yet have, or talk about your willingness to learn.

Remember!

It is not always the case that the person or team with whom you will be working will have been solely responsible for the advert, job description and person specification that have been issued. Indeed, the person who will actually be managing you may have had very little to do with that side of the process. That is why it makes sense to stress the positives – the people who compiled the advert and paperwork might not have realised the potential importance of a skill you have but which they have not mentioned; if you have a great skill that you are sure would be useful in the role, shout about it!

2.6 Managing the process

A career is so much more than a series of job titles – it forms the pattern of your life. A lawyer is paid to be articulate and patient in stressful situations, but so too is an advocate for social rights, and a bartender with a difficult customer. The point is that your job will have you using a series of skills, which rely on your skills base, your education and training and your personal qualities, and that could well be what matters to you most in the final analysis, because that is how you will actually be spending your days.

If, for even a short while, you can focus on what you would like to be doing, rather than always looking at the job title and what you will be called, you have a better chance of achieving a fulfilling career. It will also help you to be open-minded. There are so many careers out there, hundreds of which you will never have heard mentioned, but if you are clear about your skills base then you can begin to explore the careers market more fully and to better purpose.

The thing about skills is that we are developing these all the time. A minor example of this happened just this morning as one of us was making up a new document. She realised, for the first time ever, that she could create her own bullet points from images she had on her computer, rather than using the standard bullet points. Immediately she imagined how much more effective her handouts could be in future, but she also indulged in a moment's fantasy: if she were producing sales documents in-house for an estate agent, she would produce really effective house particulars, with little houses as bullet points, and if she were an administrator she could produce minutes of meetings that would catch everyone's attention ...

She stopped there, but you can see how each skill leads on to new career ideas, and we are adding to our skills inventory (see page 44) all the time. For that reason alone, do not abandon doing this once this step is complete – continue to manage the process by updating your skills inventory regularly and allowing new skills to lead you, in prospect at least, into new areas of activity.

Further reading

As part of managing the process, you may find it useful to do further research using the following recommended websites.

2.2 My skills base

What skills do I need and how do I boost them?

www.jobs.ac.uk/careers-advice/interview-tips/1337/what-are-employers-looking-for-skills-and-qualifications – This webpage focuses on the skills employers are looking for and the rest of the site will be useful to you in your search for a suitable career.

2.3 Identifying my skills

A skills inventory:

www.kent.ac.uk/careers/sk/skillsinventory.html – We have included this website earlier in the book as it really is very useful, particularly for students looking to enter the career market. This page helps you create your skills inventory.

2.4 Boosting my skills

Finding out where I need to boost my skills:

www.outcomesstar.org.uk – this explains what the Outcomes Star is and helps you create one for yourself. This is a useful and well-used tool to work out which skills you have already and which ones you need to develop.

Finding ways to boost my skills:

www.kent.ac.uk/careers/sk/skillsmenu.htm – This webpage focuses on the skills you have or will need to enter your new career.

2.5 Selling my skills

Soft skills looked for by employers and how to include them on your CV:

https://nationalcareersservice.direct.gov.uk/aboutus/newsarticles/Pages/Spotlight-SoftSkills.aspx – This website lists and explains the soft skills that employers might be looking for in their employees. Soft skills include things such as communication, decision-making and time management skills.

www.businessnewsdaily.com/2135-job-skills-resume.html – This is an article looking at how to make your CV stand out from all of the others received by an employer.

www.interview-skills.co.uk/competency-based-interviews-STAR.aspx – The STAR (situation, task, action, result) system is a good model of communication in interviews. This website gives you more information about it.

Step Three: Considering all of your options

Read this section now if:

- You are looking for a career that is different from the jobs you have had before.
- You are considering self-employment and want to know if this will suit you.
- You are ready to be self-employed but are not sure where to start.
- You would enjoy a variety of jobs to make up your ideal career.
- You would like to know how you could benefit from a portfolio career.
- You would like the skills to prepare yourself for a portfolio career.

3.1 Introduction: why does it matter?

You may have tried several jobs and found that they did not quite fit your needs and expectations. You may have found that all of those jobs suited you, but you would rather have had some variety, doing several jobs at one time. You might be frustrated by the idea of earning profit for an organisation when you could be self-employed. For any of these reasons, you could be wondering how you can find a career path that suits your individual needs better than standard employment for one firm doing one job. Most of us are drawn into the traditional system of employment without taking a step back and looking at options that will make us happier; that is why we have included this step – to give you the chance to take a little time away from the usual options, considering the wider picture.

3.2 An overview of your options

What might a non-standard career look like?

There are several non-standard career paths that you might take and there are advantages and disadvantages for each, as with traditional career paths. You may be considering self-employment, which will have benefits such as being able to manage your own time, perhaps making more money, and being able to make decisions for yourself and your business. On the other hand, being self-employed requires you to consider company insurance, tax and national insurance, as well as the risk that if you cannot work due to illness, you do not have the benefit of sick pay.

Some employers, particularly agencies, will insist that you work on a self-employed basis even if they give you regular work that you feel could be or should be a regularised job. This is so that they can avoid having to pay your tax and national insurance or offering you other benefits such as maternity leave, sick leave and so on. It might then be reasonable to ask 'why would I want to be self-employed?' For those of us who prefer to pick and choose the work we undertake, this will feel like having the freedom to do so, which will outweigh the potential disadvantages of being self-employed, whereas for others this option will not appeal at all.

> **Remember!**
>
> A career defines a large part of your life and so your response to it is likely to be emotional and linked strongly to your sense of identity. You do not have to have a rational explanation of why you would prefer to be employed by someone else, or be able to explain why that would feel claustrophobic to you. It is noticeable that people who are self-employed often say that they simply could not countenance being employed by anyone else – it is about who you are and how you feel about your life.

Another non-standard career that might appeal to you is a 'portfolio career' (see page 68); this usually involves having several job roles that you manage at one time, but the term can also refer to the careers of people who have moved from one role to another throughout their lives. For an example of the former use of the term, one of us is a college lecturer, assessor and internal quality assurer (for more than one organisation), as well as a self-employed language interpreter, freelance trainer and author. What this portfolio career allows for is management of your own time, a range of activities drawing on multiple skills and satisfying a range of passions. A variety of jobs can satisfy those people who get bored with doing the same job every day; who want to be able to earn enough from one job to support the passion that another job satisfies; who like to be autonomous; who have two or more dream careers that they would like to pursue.

Careful!

Portfolio careers are sometimes referred to as 'butterfly careers', reflecting the fact that these are the careers of people who have not stayed in one job from leaving education until retirement. The term 'butterfly career' can have negative connotations, suggesting that perhaps you are unsettled, flighty or lacking commitment. Be aware of this possibility and ensure that your CV is the best sales pitch for what you are selling rather than a lengthy note of apology for who you are.

How might a non-standard career differ from a standard career?

Firstly, a typical job will have a distinctive path for you to follow to move upwards in your career of choice; a non-standard career may need to be forged by you (which might well appeal to you). Secondly, a standard job will bring in a regular wage that you can rely on and you will be paid sick leave and have other such benefits; a non-standard career is likely to require you to invest more time and possibly money into setting yourself up. However, you may have a greater earning potential and more free time in a career path you have made yourself. Thirdly, you will be responsible for your own decision making and your own earning capacity in a non-standard career; for some this will appeal whilst for others it will be a terrifying prospect.

Remember!

If you do opt for a non-standard career, it is worth remembering that not everyone will understand what you are doing or why you are doing it. Have patience and the courage of your convictions to choose a career path that suits you.

What might be the advantages of a non-standard career path?

The following checklist will give you food for thought.

Checklist

- You might be in a stronger position to name your own terms to each employer, if you have several.
- You might be less likely to get 'stuck in a rut'.
- Very flexible working arrangements could be a realistic goal.
- You might be able to arrange your hours around a partner's commitments.
- Periods of education and training could be interwoven with other career activities.
- You could feel less tied down to one place, or one image of yourself.
- You would be in charge of your own schedule, to some extent.
- You would have more autonomy to work as you please.
- Working from home is a clear possibility.
- You might command far more money if you work on a freelance basis, or run your own company.
- You will be ready to grab each new challenge as it arises.
- You will not be constrained by having one set of work colleagues.
- You will be able to take career breaks to travel or improve your life in other ways.

Remember!

What we are outlining as advantages might not seem like advantages to you at all. For example, we could advocate 'good money' as an advantage, whereas you may not care in the least how much you earn, as long as it is a living wage. This list of advantages must therefore be taken in the spirit in which it is intended: as a guide to what some people would consider to be the advantages to this career choice, rather than the last word on the topic.

What might be the disadvantages?

Here is another checklist, this time to help you think about some of the possible pitfalls in a non-standard career path.

Checklist

- You would have less automatic security as part of one contract of employment.
- You would be more independent but also more responsible for your earnings, perhaps having to pay your own tax by completing a tax return.
- You may miss out on regular opportunities to maintain work friendships; you might be lonely.

- Promotion may pass you by if you are not in an organisation long, or there on a freelance basis.
- If you are self-employed you might have to push for each income increment you receive.
- There might perhaps be less security of position and income.
- Self-employment often means no automatic holiday pay and similar entitlements.
- You could miss out on new career possibilities if you are not seen as a long-standing, regular member of the team.
- In times of recession your earning potential might diminish.
- Your status will depend upon how well you sell yourself, rather than coming automatically along with a job title.
- You might have to 'follow the money' and work long hours at times.

Remember!

Not all of the pros and cons listed in these two sections will be relevant to you; we know that you might not need to concern yourself with income security, for example, and if this is the case you can happily ignore that possible disadvantage.

Am I the right person for this?

Only you can decide that, but the lists above will give you some clues. As well as noting if you responded positively to the list of advantages, also consider your reaction to the list of possible disadvantages. If you did not really see these as disadvantages, either because they do not apply or because they are not of great importance to you, then you will probably want to look more closely at a non-standard career path.

3.3 Self-employment

What should I consider first in thinking about self-employment?

The first thing to consider is whether you have the temperament to be self-employed. It may sound like hard work and we can safely say that it is but we believe that the advantages outweigh the disadvantages. That is our opinion from our experiences. Your friends and family may have their own experiences of self-employment to share with you. No matter what advice you get, you must make sure that the decision is yours. We love writing lists and so we would recommend that you write a pros and cons list to help you decide if this is the right move for you. Why not be proactive and write a series of plans and lists now?

Success checklist

✓ Write out a brief overview (no more than 300 words) of what your self-employment would entail. This could range from an outline of a good idea you have had for your own business, to a draft plan of how you intend to work as a freelancer.

(Continued)

Careful!

There is a clear difference between starting your own business (in which you might be selling services and/or products, perhaps employing others and taking on business premises such as a shop, café or office) and working as a self-employed freelancer, doing the same job as you would normally have done as an employed member of staff but working as an independent entity, negotiating your own terms and managing your own finances.

(Continued)

✓ Produce a list to remind yourself of the top six reasons why you want to follow this path.
✓ Now write up a list of the six challenges that you will face – that is, the six main disadvantages that you can see to this plan.
✓ Review these lists to confirm that you still want to go ahead before you move on to the next task.
✓ Look at your master CV (you can learn how to produce this in Step Six, page 115) and decide whether you have what it takes to succeed in your plan, or whether you need to undertake more training or take any other action that will give you the best chance of success.
✓ Talk to people in your networks (for more on your networks see Step Five, page 92) and share with them your overview – be open to other ideas and suggestions.

(Continued)

Careful!

Getting carried away with your idea and failing to listen to your network contacts is the biggest mistake you could make at this stage. You do not have to slavishly follow every piece of advice you are offered, but you do need to listen and consider the wisdom of others.

(Continued)

✓ Revise your plan in the light of your network discussions.
✓ Make a business plan so that you are confident you can afford to take this step.

(Continued)

Top tip

The thought of making a business plan can, understandably, be scary if you have never produced one before. Think of it this way – it is no more than a means by which you can predict, as accurately as possible, how much you will earn and how you plan to earn this over a period of time. For a start-up business this would typically be two to three years, whereas for a freelancer it might only be for the first year.

(Continued)

✓ Research and possibly set up anything that you might legally be obliged to do, such as informing HMRC (the tax office) and preparing to pay your own National Insurance Contributions. You will also need to arrange insurance (Public Liability Insurance if you are working in an industry that involves dealing with the public) and you might want to register with any relevant professional bodies.

(Continued)

Remember!

Not all government bodies simply want to take a share of your profits. You might be entitled to government grants, social benefits and other support whilst you set up your business – you can find out more at your local government offices or online.

(Continued)

✓ Your business plan will have shown you that the overall project is feasible financially, but you will still want to check at the outset that you have enough money (or you have access to enough finance) to be able to start up as self-employed. You may find that you do not get a substantial enough income in the first few months to be able to cover your outlays.

(Continued)

Top tip

Not having quite enough money day to day (namely insufficient cashflow) is not a sign of failure as long as you have foreseen it. You might, for example, need money for some initial training, or registering with a professional body or register, or your work might be seasonal – all of these can be foreseen in your business plan.

(Continued)

✓ Make a clear plan so that know what you are going to do, and by when you are going to achieve your goals.

(Continued)

Top tip

Build some leeway into your plans by going for a lower estimate on income than you would like and a slightly higher estimate on outgoings. It is far more comfortable to overachieve and be able to put some money aside than to feel that your plans are going awry and that you are failing in some way.

(Continued)

✓ As you move towards self-employment, take the time to review your plans regularly, making sure that you are on the right track.
✓ If things do not quite go according to plan, do not ignore the problem. Use your network contacts to help you visualise where things are going wrong and come up with ideas on how to fix these.

Remember!

A business problem is rarely resolved by ignoring it, and it is easier to fix the problem and move forward if you have supporters on your side prepared to help you through. Include your bank's business advisor in your list of network contacts.

What does a business plan look like?

At this point we had considered working through a business plan with you in detail, but the more we discussed it the more we came to realise that there were far too many variants to make this a useful exercise for our readers. Then, luckily, we typed 'free business plan templates' into an internet search engine and so many hits popped up that we felt confident in advising you to do just the same thing (see www.princes-trust.org.uk/need_help/enterprise_programme/explore_where_to_start/business_plans/business_plan_templates. aspx? – this was one of the first websites to come up and it is a reliable source for you to use).

Careful!

Avoid being led into spending money on business planning until you are certain that you need to make that investment. In these early stages, especially as you are deciding whether you even want to make this move, your bank may well offer significant amounts of advice for free (either in person or through free software), the tax office (HMRC) website includes plenty of valuable advice and guidance and there are HMRC offices from which you can obtain help. Check out free help online (making sure that it really is free before you commit to anything) and also consider your local Chamber of Commerce or government-funded small business start-up schemes and centres.

How can I ensure that my business plan will work?

By avoiding the pitfalls that loom ahead of you.

Success checklist

✓ Be as accurate as you can – time spent researching the likely market for your skills or product will not be wasted.

✓ Be clear with yourself about the terms you will be using in your business plan, and make sure that others are equally clear. If you are talking about a 'financial period', is this a month? Three months? A year?

(Continued)

Careful!

The terms used in self-employment and business can seem to be almost deliberately confusing at times. For example, your 'income' might no longer be the same as it would be in employment. It may refer to the whole amount of money you have taken in, before you take off your expenses (also called your 'turnover'). Ask for guidance if you are confused by the terminology and then help your supporters to understand what you are talking about as you seek their assistance with your plan.

(Continued)

✓ Use your own experience – if you are going to become a freelancer in a familiar field you can make well-informed predictions; avoid assuming that more or less work will be available in the area overall just because you are freelance.

✓ Be cautious but not scared – lower estimates of likely income make sense because they will give you a buffer, but make sure that you are not letting yourself become too pessimistic as this might put you off altogether.

✓ Use your contacts – your fellow experts in a field can review your plan with you to confirm that it is realistic; this might be a good way to alert them to your project so that they can put work or clients your way.

(Continued)

(Continued)

✓ Rather than just making a promise to yourself to review your plan against your activities from time to time, actually write this into your plan. Time slips by at an astonishing rate when you work for yourself, so 'review' written firmly in your plan from time to time is going to be essential.

✓ In business, 'turnover' is rarely the same as 'profit'. Try not to be so excited about your turnover that you forget that your outgoings must be deducted from this before you get to a profit figure, and that your drawings from the business (this will be your actual income) will have to take into account your tax liability.

(Continued)

Careful!

Always be wary of anyone who talks loudly about their income but then does not seem to know the difference between turnover (what they take in) and profit (what is left after they have paid everything out). If they also seem to have no clue about 'pre-tax profit' (that is, what they have made before they pay tax on it), be even more suspicious of how financially sound their business is likely to be.

(Continued)

✓ Use your business plan as the basis for further planning. A three-year plan could be expanded to a set of more detailed plans showing three month periods of activity. Planning to produce a certain amount of income in each of those three months will require a plan showing the timescale of how the work will be carried out, and a marketing plan of how you are going to bring the work in.

✓ Your plan is not yet reality – see it as your vision of the next few months or years, and then keep accurate records of what actually happened for your tax accounts.

✓ Your plan is also not a magic money spell. You cannot decide how much you want to earn and then finesse your plan so that it unrealistically shows that this exact figure is going to be your profit. People make this mistake far more often than you might expect, and they often have no idea that they are doing it, so make sure that you divorce your need for a certain amount of money from your plan to make a profit.

✓ Do not worry if your plan is less precise the further into the future it goes – this is often inevitable and your reviews will allow you to add detail as time moves on.

How could I use short-term self-employment to my advantage?

Self-employment will help you acquire additional skills that you can use to impress future employers. We talked earlier about drawing the skills out of an experience and this is a perfect example of when to do it. You will find that during your time as a self-employed individual you will develop some or all of the skills listed below.

Success checklist

✓ Time management
✓ Project management
✓ Communication skills
✓ Financial skills
✓ Planning skills
✓ The ability to review and evaluate actions
✓ Marketing skills (you have been selling yourself as a self-employed person!)
✓ Budgeting acumen
✓ Risk assessment (this could be simply weighing up the benefits and risks of taking on a job or project)
✓ Management skills (you may have managed other people as well as your time and budget)
✓ Team skills

The above list is by no means exhaustive and you may also have developed specialist skills that will be attractive to a potential employer, so use this as a starter and then expand it to reflect your situation. This can then feed into your master CV (see Step Six, page 115 for more on this).

Remember!

Do not forget that employers will understand that being self-employed takes courage and the confidence to make decisions, so it can be an excellent selling point.

What if an employer offers me a self-employment contract?

You will need to find out what they will take responsibility for in terms of insurance and what they expect from you. You should expect to be paid more as you will be responsible for your own tax and National Insurance. You will need to find out if you will be charging them travel costs (you are entitled to decide this). Do not forget that as you are self-employed, you have the right to refuse work. You will need to either agree to their Terms and Conditions or create your own, that they will then sign as evidence that they will abide by them. Make sure you have a clear procedure from being offered the work, accepting it, carrying it out, and invoicing for it. You will also need to consider what would happen should you be ill or need to cancel work.

Careful!

Being offered the chance to work as a freelancer by an employer will often represent a winning situation for you both. You might gain more work and flexibility at a genuinely improved rate of return for your efforts, and your employer would lose some of the administration and costs involved in employing you. There is thus no need to be too suspicious about an offer like this, but if you feel that you are being coerced into accepting such a contract, talk to your union or professional body, contact your local Citizens Advice Bureau and/or work with your colleagues to negotiate with the employer.

Where should I go for more help and advice?

As we have already mentioned, avoid help that is chargeable until you are sure that you want to pay for it. If you have a high profit or complicated financial affairs you might want to engage an accountant, but in the first instance, try centrally funded contacts such as those on the checklist.

Success checklist

✓ HMRC (Her Majesty's Revenue and Customs – the tax office) gives advice on income tax, self-employment, various business taxes and VAT. The site is impressively practical, sharing guidance on what records to keep and how to ensure that you do things correctly. The website is www.gov.uk/government/organisations/hm-revenue-customs

✓ www.princes-trust.org.uk/need_help/enterprise_programme.aspx is aimed at people setting up their own business between the ages of 18 and 30.

✓ www.smallbusiness.co.uk and other similar sites have advice about setting up your own business. Just make sure that you are not lured into paying for anything unexpected.

✓ www.fsb.org.uk (the Federation of Small Businesses) will be able to give you legal advice, insurance cover, support in employing others and much more.

✓ www.isbe.org.uk (the Institute for Small Business and Entrepreneurship) has some useful information on its website for starting up and succeeding in your small business.

✓ www.citizensadvice.org.uk gives you a checklist of all the things you will need to know to be successfully self-employed.

✓ www.gov.uk/working-for-yourself gives information about what you need to consider when setting up as a self-employed person.

3.4 Further study

Why might I do further academic study?

If you have been perusing the job market for a while and struggling to get into a new career, it is prudent to think about returning to education to upskill. Academic study will give you the chance to gain new skills and further your expertise in an area that might be beneficial to your dream career. You should plan carefully what you are going to study to ensure that this will help you into employment.

Careful!

It can be tempting to undertake the first academic course you find simply because you cannot think what else to do. This can lead to some fruitful and enjoyable days ahead, but it is best to study something for which you have a real interest or passion. If you are less than passionate about the topic you plan to study you need to be certain that it will lead directly to an improved career situation.

What about vocational training?

If you think that academic study will not particularly assist you into your new career, and you have no great desire to study in that way, you should consider vocational training. Vocational training tends to be designed to fit in with your work hours and can be significantly cheaper. If you are already in work, you may find that your workplace will support you either by giving you time off to attend classes or with a financial contribution. Vocational training is designed to give you a qualification tied to a specific career; on the other hand, academic study could start off being very broad and end up being very narrow in terms of a research field or area of study and might not be tied directly to the daily functions of a career. (Complete Exercise #9 at the back of the book to help you evaluate what training you would benefit from at this stage in your career journey.)

Top tip

Whatever you are studying, either academically or vocationally, remember that you are improving your general, professional skills base all the time. If this is not obvious

(Continued)

(Continued)

to you from the course content, take time to analyse (as you did with your skills inventory on page 152) what you are gaining beyond your subject area. This could include time keeping, articulating an argument, team working, report writing and so forth.

What about professional development activities?

Professional development can too easily be overlooked when you are plotting your career path. This is largely because it might be informal training or, indeed, not be the result of a training course at all. Redesigning the website of your local sports organisation, for example, might be what you do in your spare time, but it may represent significant professional development as you learn about and put into practice design methodologies, sales techniques and web design principles. You might also be attending conferences, webinars, workshops, or short courses (perhaps supported by e-learning) that seem to you to be minor and may not be undertaken as a result of a job, but these need to be recorded in your experience and skills inventories as part of your path towards a great career.

In some professions there is an expectation to develop professionally and so professional bodies and organisations will be set up to deliver training or signpost you towards local training opportunities. You may be required by your employer to do a certain amount of professional development over the course of a year. It is certainly worth doing to keep up to date and it also shows your employer that you are keen to learn.

Careful!

If you are in work and your employers provide you with a significant amount of training, they may ask you to agree that you will then stay with them for a set amount of time or you will be liable to pay back some or all of the cost of the training.

Where should I go next?

A methodical approach to this aspect of your career development can be beneficial in that it can spur you on to action and help you plan for the best use of your time and resources.

Success checklist

✓ Ask your current employer, if you have one, if there are any courses being run in your organisation that you can undertake.
✓ Check with your professional body whether it has any courses you could join.
✓ Check with your local training providers as these can sometimes offer workshops or public lectures or conferences that could benefit you.
✓ When you go for interviews, ask if the organisation offers professional development opportunities.
✓ Check the job adverts you have been looking at to see if there are any areas you could start developing to improve your chances of success.

You might have noticed that we have referred to your professional body in this step, and this may seem alien to your way of thinking. Many people have never joined a professional body, nor really seen a need to, but these can be an excellent source of information and offer good chances to network. Browsing through some websites will take only a few minutes of your time and will at least give you the chance to make an informed decision about whether joining would be worth your while. For UK bodies, the government directory is a good place to start (www.gov.uk/government/publications/professional-bodies-approved-for-tax-relief-list-3/approved-professional-organisations-and-learned-societies), but a general web browse can also bring up some of the smaller, but often equally useful, bodies and professional groups.

What are the potential benefits to further study?

The benefits are primarily yours but they extend to future employers and colleagues too. By embarking on further study, you are improving your skills and knowledge in the area you wish to work in; this means you are more likely to get into the career you dream of and you could also be commanding a higher salary. From an employer's perspective, you are a more expert employee who has demonstrated a keen interest in the area and shown you are interested in the field. Your new colleagues will benefit from your expertise and you will find that more doors open for you.

What might be the pitfalls?

Further study comes at a cost. You may be eligible for funding, and although it can be tedious trawling through websites about bursaries and funding opportunities, this could prove worthwhile in the long run.

Once you are doing a course of study you are committed to it and there is a risk that you will either become lax in your pursuit of that perfect career or you will not be able to grab the opportunities as they arise. As long as you are aware of the pitfalls, you should certainly contemplate what additional qualifications will do for your CV and your chances of getting into a perfect career.

The rumour is true – you can be *over-qualified* for a job. Unfortunately, if you have a qualification far higher than the role demands, you could find that prospective employers feel uncomfortable about giving you the job as they are concerned that you will get bored, demand a higher salary, or be using the job as a stopgap before bouncing off into a better paid career. There are exceptions to the rule and if you can explain to them why you are going for the job that will help your case enormously.

Top tip

Being over-qualified for a job does not mean that you have to shout about it to everyone. We have known several academic doctors who undertook a PhD because they knew they would enjoy the challenge. They had no intention of pursuing their academic interest any further and they have made a positive decision to leave the title 'Dr' off their CVs because they believe that it might confuse or concern potential employers. Your CV is your sales pitch, and this means only including on it those qualifications, skills and experience that you believe are marketable in your target career area.

3.5 A portfolio career

What is a portfolio career?

As mentioned earlier, you could be thinking about a portfolio career, wherein you pursue more than one career.

Top tip

http://portfoliocareers.net is a useful website with information on books and some answers to questions about portfolio careers.

Are there different types of portfolio career?

Yes. In a portfolio career you might be managing two or more careers in parallel with each other at the same time (we call this a parallel portfolio career).

This can be exhausting and exhilarating in equal measure. This is a rather more common phenomenon in the UK than it used to be, and if you are working here for the first time you might find that this career pattern is more familiar here than in your home country.

The second type is what we refer to as a longitudinal portfolio career, which means that you plan to have more than one career over your working life; for some people this means planning decades in advance.

Why would I consider this?

There was a time when people would plan to be in the same job for their entire working lives; now there is a lot more mobility in the career market. You may feel that you have several careers that you feel passionate about and so would like to be able to explore all of your options. There is a benefit to having a portfolio career in the sense that you are able to have job security from a number of careers, allowing you to relax safe in the knowledge that if one does not fare so well, you can rely on an income and opportunities from the other(s).

The other reason that you might consider a portfolio career is to allow you the time to do activities outside of work. For example, you might work and earn money half of the year to be able to afford to volunteer or work on a lower salary for the second half of the year.

A parallel or longitudinal career portfolio can be the prudent choice. Recent research, although disparate, seems to suggest that businesses have to replace approximately half of their employees over a four- to five-year period, half of their mid-level managers each five- to six-year period, and about half of their senior executives each seven- to eight-year period. We are no longer in a position to expect to have a job for life. You will find that many of your colleagues will be building up their skills and preparing for when they need to transition to their new career. You will benefit by doing this also, so as to make that transition as smooth as possible. (To find out if a portfolio career is for you, complete Exercise #10 at the back of the book.)

How could I make a more detailed plan for a portfolio career?

Complete Exercise #11 at the back of the book to help you achieve a detailed plan for a portfolio career. You may do this in conjunction with Exercise #10.

Both of the exercises above are challenging and are going to take time and effort to complete. Use your networks so that you can talk your ideas through with your supporters, who will offer you reality checks as well as encouragement, and take your time. Planning time will not be wasted time when you are making such a major decision.

How could a portfolio career help me when I go to job interviews?

The skills that you develop over the course of one career are considered valuable to employers, so just imagine how delighted they will be by the broad range of skills you will have developed over a portfolio career! You will have a wide range of experiences and skills to talk about in your interviews, and you will find it easier to cope with potential anxiety over interviews as by then you will have built up your confidence through dealing with a range of people in a variety of careers.

Remember!

Experience is important and a wide range of experience is even better. Employers like to hire people who are experienced because they already have skills and they need less training. If you are continuing to do a multitude of jobs as part of your portfolio career then an employer may need you to outline why you are going for the job they are offering and how you are going to fit it in. Be prepared to make your CV an excellent sales pitch for what you have to offer and move to a functional CV (outlined in Step Six, page 113) if you think that this would make the best case to a potential employer.

Is there a downside to this move?

You could have an outlay during the setting-up of your portfolio career and this could have an impact financially, emotionally, physically and mentally. If you are aiming for a job or several jobs you will have the stress of applying, interviewing for and starting a new job. Potentially, you will be either doing this process several times in a short space of time, or you will be doing this multiple times over your career, or you will be becoming self-employed. If you are self-employed you might be doing your own marketing, setting up your own terms and conditions, arranging your finances, keeping your own accounts, meeting with clients, chasing up clients, invoicing, meeting professional standards, and hoping that when you go to bed late you will have a smile on your face because you have had a thrilling day doing exactly what you love.

3.6 Managing the process

You will probably have noticed that each section of Step Three requires you to think deeply about your goals and values and how you can achieve or fulfil them. This is going to be an ongoing process and at times it will be tough, as you make life-changing decisions in the hope and belief that you are on the right course. Setting targets for yourself can relieve much of the pressure that this can entail, and if they are SMART targets you can reassure yourself that you are on track and on time. Reviewing your SMART targets regularly allows you to finesse your plans in response to moving circumstances and perhaps your changing needs and ambitions over time.

Success checklist

SMART targets are as follows:

- ✓ **S**pecific – make sure you are precise in defining your target.
- ✓ **M**easurable – use active verbs to ensure that you can measure your success. For example, rather than saying 'I will understand how to put together a business plan', use 'I will put together a business plan and ask someone with more experience to review it with me'.
- ✓ **A**chievable/attainable – ensure that there are no barriers in the way to you achieving your target. If there are insurmountable barriers, change the target.
- ✓ **R**ealistic/relevant – it is important that your target is within your reach and relevant to what you want to do. You will feel demotivated if you expected to be able to run a marathon by the end of the week even though you had never done long-distance running before!
- ✓ **T**ime-bound/timely – do not let your targets drag on as this is a drain on your energy and enthusiasm for the whole project; also make sure that are carrying out activities at the most appropriate time for your goals.

Careful!

It is easy to be impressed by the hype around SMART targets, believing that they could change your life. Such is the enthusiasm for them that, as you can see above, there is disagreement over what each letter of the acronym means ('Should it be 'realistic' or is 'relevant' better?' people ask). You can even develop your planning into the creation of SMARTER targets, once you have decided whether the extra 'E' stands for 'evaluate', 'enthusiastic' or 'ethical' and whether the final 'R' is 're-do', 'recorded' or 'rewarded'. There is no doubt that this method offers you a powerful planning tool, but avoid being so caught up in the planning that you forget to actually move forward.

Further reading

As part of managing the process, you may find it useful to do further research using these recommended websites:

3.3 Self-employment

Where to go for more information and advice:

www.gov.uk/government/organisations/hm-revenue-customs – This is the government website where you can register your financial accounts, find out about the National Insurance and tax you will need to pay, and pay your taxes. It also offers information about being self-employed in the UK.

www.princes-trust.org.uk/need_help/enterprise_programme.aspx – There are plenty of organisations that will offer bursaries to help people set up their own businesses or get training.

www.princes-trust.org.uk/need_help/enterprise_programme/explore_where_to_start/business_plans/business_plan_templates.aspx? – This page of the Prince's Trust website offers free business plan templates.

www.smallbusiness.co.uk – This website gives you important information about all of the legal considerations in setting up as self-employed or employing others.

www.fsb.org.uk – This is the Federation of Small Businesses website. You could sign up as a member to get certain benefits such as employment law advice and financial health checks.

www.isbe.org.uk – This is the website for the Institute for Small Business and Entrepreneurship. Membership of this will offer you a useful network if you are starting up or running a small business.

www.citizensadvice.org.uk – This is a useful website to give you advice whether you are employed, self-employed, an employer or looking for work.

www.gov.uk/working-for-yourself – This is a government website offering useful information about what working for yourself entails legally.

3.4 Further study

Where to go for more training and skills development advice:

www.gov.uk/career-skills-and-training – This is a useful hub of information about further training that might be of interest to you, as well as referring you to different possible funding sources.

Finding a professional body that may be able to advise you on further training requirements and opportunities:

www.gov.uk/government/publications/professional-bodies-approved-for-tax-relief-list-3/approved-professional-organisations-and-learned-societies – This is a list of professional bodies that have been approved for tax relief. It is a useful starting point for finding professional bodies that you may want to join.

3.5 A portfolio career

Article about portfolio careers and what you need to consider:

www.jobs.ac.uk/careers-advice/careers-advice/1545/is-portfolio-working-for-you – This website gives you some more information about portfolio careers and what to do next.

Further reading:

http://portfoliocareers.net – This is a useful website focused on portfolio careers. There is also a section for further reading.

Step Four: Researching the career market

4.1 Introduction: why does it matter?

You are reading this book and that is proof enough that you want to make the best career choices and then succeed as quickly and efficiently as possible. That means not only making the right choices but also transforming yourself from a passive recipient of information to an active seeker after opportunities. Simply checking jobs websites or buying newspapers and journals to look at the careers sections is not going to be enough, you will need to find the opportunities that are there, but lingering just below the gaze of an idle observer. That is what this step is about – making the most of your time and effort and – as we are repeatedly urging you to do – taking control of your own fate.

4.2 Deciphering the career market

Where do I start?

Brainstorm, brainstorm, brainstorm. If you think too deeply about one career you are in danger of losing your overview of the available options, and if you begin to consider all of the careers that are on offer, you might give up on the basis that the choice is just too vast. Working with friends and supporters will help; keeping going until you feel you have exhausted the reasonable possibilities for you is going to be key. (Go to Exercise #12 for more on this area.)

So where next?

You now have a list of possible careers and you have worked on skills and experience inventories so you have a good sense of what you have to offer. Most importantly, you have a clear idea of what motivates and demotivates you and an overall pattern for how you would like your career to unfold.

Now, to action! You need to find out more. For each of the careers you have identified, produce a brief outline that includes salary, entry requirements, future training opportunities and suchlike.

Success checklist

Try to be bold, unrelenting and inclusive here, using all of these resources at once:

- ✓ Careers/recruitment fairs.
- ✓ Jobcentre Plus.
- ✓ Recruitment agencies specialising in your field, but also more general job agencies.
- ✓ Professional bodies.
- ✓ Specialist print and online media in your areas of interest.
- ✓ Your own networks – what have your contacts heard recently?
- ✓ Journals, newspapers and magazines – both in print and online.
- ✓ Professional network sites such as LinkedIn™.
- ✓ Social media – is there a potential professional support network already waiting to offer ideas?
- ✓ Job adverts – both for the careers you want and for similar but not obviously perfect careers that you might explore.

Once I know what I might want to do, how do I start researching it?

Once you have compiled a list of potential careers, you might want to research those that you have put a question mark beside. Be systematic in your approach here as you could spend hours trawling through websites and information about each career and feel exhausted and overwhelmed by the end of it. We recommend that you use the Success Checklist below to help focus your research.

Success checklist

Use one piece of paper per career opportunity so that you can then lay these side by side to compare them. Keep your lists short and aim to spend a maximum of half an hour on each career you are researching.

✓ Job title
✓ Bullet point the responsibilities
✓ What is the average salary for this job?
✓ Are there opportunities within the local area to do this role?
✓ What are the entry requirements into this career?
✓ What are the training opportunities?
✓ What are the advantages and disadvantages of doing this job?

Once you have your lists you should go away from these, as you may feel more positively about the one you have most recently researched as it is still fresh in your mind. You might find it beneficial to have a supporter or mentor with you during this next process. For what to do next, go to Exercise #13 at the back of the book.

How do I use my research to get interviews?

You will already have done some research into career opportunities in your chosen field and so now you need to start homing in on the specific organisations that you could work for. Go to the websites of potential employers and check if they have any vacancies. If they do, you can go through the application process that they have in place. If they do not have any advertised on their website, this does not necessarily mean that they have no opportunities there, so it is worth calling them to ask.

Keep a list of all of the companies that you research so that you can do two things: firstly, you can keep going back to them if you like what they do or you can rule them out if you do not like the company, and secondly, you can see just how much work you have done and congratulate yourself for it.

What about cold calling on the phone?

Cold calling can work fantastically well in many instances. Simply picking up the phone and asking whether there are any vacancies in your area of interest can mean that you find yourself in an instant interview. We can help you through your first experience of this if you go to Exercise #14 at the back of the book.

Should I cold call in person?

If you are feeling determined, walking into an organisation's place of business can be the most effective way to secure a positon there. Again, we will lead you through how this works in Exercise #15 at the back of the book.

Do not be disheartened if you are told that there are no opportunities opening up at the moment – this is still an important conversation. The so-called 'hidden job market' is all about people recommending people rather than advertising in the hope that a suitable person will simply appear. The person to whom you are talking might not be able to offer you a job, but may well know someone who can.

Can you cold call online?

Yes, and the principles remain exactly the same – an email to a named individual in an organisation, with a nice, open question so as to begin a conversation about what you can offer the organisation and the opportunities that might be available to you.

It is important to remember that you are asking for something, as well as offering something, so if an email goes unanswered it would not be good practice simply to keep badgering the same contact for a reply. Instead, either change tack and contact someone else in the organisation or ring your contact and ask when might be a good time for you to call back for a chat.

You may have noticed that we have referred several times to 'a chat' or 'chatting' – this is indicative of the level of informality that tends to work well in these situations. You are not entering into a highly formal negotiation, but neither are you having a good old gossip; you are taking a few minutes out of someone's day to talk informally about what you have to offer that could benefit that person's organisation.

What is 'warm calling'?

Warm calling is far easier than cold calling, but it does not necessarily offer you as wide-ranging a set of opportunities. You warm call an organisation when you are aware that they have career openings. This might, for example, be because you have seen a job advert and potential applicants have been invited to call for a 'job chat'. It might be that you have seen adverts for positions that are similar to your field but not ideally suited to your skills set – this sort of call allows you to ask if the firm is also planning to recruit in your area.

Warm calling can happen on the phone or online (either by email or in a chat room set up by the company or recruitment agency) and one golden rule applies to either of these situations: never, ever, ask anyone 'Can you tell me something about the job?' The obvious answer to this is 'No. I am a busy person – read the advert or job description and then call me back when you have a real question to ask.' People really do react that strongly against this type of anodyne question, so instead you need to have a well-prepared set of queries.

As we will mention when we discuss interviews in Step Seven (see page 127), if you are asked to call for an informal chat about an opportunity, this could, in effect, be a first interview. You will therefore be judged not just on what you say, but on the questions you ask, so make sure that these reflect your interest in this opportunity and your research into the organisation.

You will be making a warm call to someone who is either expecting people to call for a job chat, or has already been told by a contact that you might be calling, or is involved in recruitment in an organisation and so is used to dealing with these calls. Use this to your advantage by being ready to talk about the scope of possibilities that may be about to open up before you – allow it to become a proper conversation.

Top tip

There is one absolute rule for any form of direct calling – always, always focus on what you can do for the organisation, rather than what this opportunity can do for you. Why you want the job will come up from time to time, of course, but even then you can focus on aspects of the job (such as training in new areas, or having the chance to develop your sales skills, or taking the opportunity to travel for the firm) that offer a benefit.

4.3 Some practicalities to consider

Why should I be thinking about practicalities now?

As you research the career market you will be gathering information, probably at an alarming rate. As your notes on telephone calls pile up, and your research material on organisation begins to build, you can feel overwhelmed. Instead of allowing this to happen to you, you can use these early stages to take control and begin on your decision making. None of the factors we mention here are necessarily deal breakers in terms of your career choices, but you might want to factor these into your thinking as you begin to make choices about which opportunities to pursue with a passion and which to consider with perhaps just a little more caution.

Is travelling far a good idea?

Do not forget that travelling long distances adds hours to your working day. If you would have to travel a long way to be able to get into the career that you are aiming for, you may decide that doing so is worthwhile. However, we would recommend that you undertake the journey before deciding whether it is a good idea or not; the theory of a 45-minute train journey is different from the practicality of actually getting onto a busy train that has been delayed by 15 minutes and is full of people who are stressed about getting to work late. If you then have no seat and so are standing and cramped for those 45 minutes, you may find the journey even less appealing.

It has become increasingly popular for organisations to offer employees a chance to work from home at least part of the time. This saves the organisation on travel expense claims, they can save space at work, and their employees tend to be more productive as they have not had a stressful journey into work that has made them miserable and preoccupied for half of the morning. You could check this with your potential employer as part of the recruitment negotiations.

Remember!

When you are considering how far you are willing to travel, you should calculate how much time each week you will spend travelling and also how much money it will cost you. With the cost of travel going up, you may find that the job paying more which is further away actually leaves you with less of a financial benefit.

Can zero-hours contracts work well?

Despite all of the controversy around zero-hours contracts, there is no doubt that these can work very well for some people, but they can also be a way for employers to exploit their employees. Given the potential pitfalls of zero-hours contracts we would suggest that, as a rule, a standard contract is likely to be suitable for you (it will offer you security of income and other standard and well-regulated employee benefits) but that you might consider a zero-hours contract under the following circumstances.

Checklist

- You are looking for temporary work to gain some cash ready for your next move.
- You are running a portfolio career and need to fill in occasionally with some money-earning activity.
- You want to gain some vital experience in a field so that you can be successful in your hunt for the perfect career.
- You would prefer to be in a position to negotiate your hours on a weekly or daily basis, rather than committing to fixed hours on a long-term basis.
- You need to take a break away from your existing career and would like to earn some money whilst you consider your options.
- You are working away from your home country and need to raise some money for a few weeks until you get your career bearings.
- You believe that some zero-hours work would give you useful contacts to increase the efficacy of your professional networks.

Careful!

Just because a zero-hours contract might suit you under some of the circumstances we have listed here, we are not suggesting that you should necessarily agree to such a contract just because you fall into one of these categories. Take into account all of your circumstances and the details of the contract being offered and take advice if you are still unsure.

Can I ask for a job share?

Yes, you can, whether or not the job has been advertised as suitable for a job share, but you must prepare well so as to make your case effectively. If the job is within an organisation for which you already work, you will be in a good position to explain how you see the role working as a job share. If you have a job share partner in mind, apply together and make a firm case as to how you would divide the hours and, more importantly, how you could do as good a job together as a single person filling the vacancy.

It is worth noting that job shares are often highly successful, for good reason. They can offer continuity of service, easier coverage for sick leave, great energy from happy employees, and two different approaches to each new challenge. They also offer two professionals, each of whom might wish to move to a full-time role in future, so a company has the chance to work with trusted colleagues fulfilling new roles rather than recruiting afresh.

We mention this as a way to demonstrate to you that you need not be apologetic about wanting or needing a job share, but you do need to make a convincing case. If you are already in a job share and are looking to move to a new organisation, it might help your case if your current boss or a colleague was prepared to talk to any potential employers about how successful your current job share has been.

Undertake some research on your target organisation before you begin discussions about job sharing – an employer with plenty of experience of the practicalities of job sharing is more likely to be enthusiastic about this possibility, whereas an employer who is new to the idea might need more reassurance.

Careful!

Do not confuse job *sharing* (where the hours dedicated to a job are split between employees) and job *splitting* (where specific tasks in a role are divided between employees). Either or both of these might appeal to you, but you need to be clear about which of these you are discussing.

How open to new prospects should I be?

The answer to this question really depends on your personality. Kolb's Experiential Learning Theory may be a useful tool for you to work out whether you would be open to new prospects and, if not, how to prepare yourself to be more open to them. You must go through all stages of the cycle to have a well-rounded approach. However, most people will feel that they fall into one or two of the categories. Once you know which category you are most aligned with, you will then be able to tailor your work and career search to suit you better. You will also be able to identify your weaknesses and work on them. For example, if you think that you do the 'reflective observation' most often, then you know that you would prefer to watch how someone else plans for a meeting first, and from there reflect on how well it worked before attempting to plan your own meeting. You may also find that the 'active experimentation' really stresses you out as jumping in before really thinking or reflecting on it is against your nature. We have outlined the four areas below. (To see an image of the cycle, go to www.simplypsychology.org/learning-kolb.html)

Concrete Experience (feeling) This is when you are actually going through an experience. You may not be doing anything other than 'feeling'. For example, you may experience someone cutting your hair.

Reflective Observation (watching) This is when you are watching someone else do something and reflecting on what and how they are doing it. For example, watching the hairdresser cutting your hair and seeing how it is combed and styled.

Abstract Conceptualisation (thinking) Thinking about what *could* happen. For example, thinking about what would happen if you cut your own hair and how you might go about doing it.

Active Experimentation (doing) Jumping in and doing something. For example, cutting your own or someone else's hair.

These exist in a cycle so that you might go through all of them without necessarily acknowledging that you are doing this. However, we tend to fit into categories in this cycle depending on our preferences. For example, you might be the type of person who would be 'Diverging', which means that you prefer to feel and watch; you would experience a haircut and enjoy watching what the hairdresser or barber was doing.

If you were the type of person who would prefer to watch someone else having their hair cut and consider what would happen if you cut your own hair or had a go at cutting their hair then you would come under 'Assimilating'.

Maybe you like to think about an activity and then have a go. In this case, we can link it to thinking about how you would cut someone's hair and then try it out, without watching someone else doing this first. In which case, you would come under 'Converging'.

Finally, you may prefer to go through an experience and then do it yourself. For example, you have your own hair cut and then go on to cut someone else's hair.

People confronted with this theory often say that they fit into two or even more of these categories depending on the situations they find themselves in. This is absolutely fine, it just means that the situation is influencing their actions.

For the purposes of your job search, you should work out which of these you are so that you can give yourself the best chance to accept new challenges and be open to new prospects. For example, if you are a 'diverging' personality then you would find it very hard to be told to 'have a go', but you could prepare yourself by going through the experience and watching someone else do it first. So if you were asked by an employer to lead a meeting, you would find that task more palatable if you had already sat in on meetings and watched other people chair them.

If you are asked by your potential employer how good you are at taking up new challenges, it would look very good if you could explain how best you handle new challenges, relating it to a theory such as this. You could plan some answers to the questions you believe are likely to come up in interview. For example, if you suspect that the fairly new and dynamic company you are interviewing at is likely to ask you about how you manage change, you could plan to refer to this theory to support your answer and come up with the following: 'I am a reflective observer according to Kolb's Experiential Cycle and so I would watch my colleagues or manager dealing with a new system to be absolutely sure that I was able to take it on with accuracy and enthusiasm.'

How much should I compromise?

There is a fine balance that must be struck when negotiating a compromise. On the one side you have resting your sense of worth, your job satisfaction and happiness, your values and your needs. On the other side you have your employer's business needs. You should be able to compromise enough so that everyone is satisfied but not so much that one party feels they have lost. Very few of us are confident when it comes to compromising, either compromising too much or not budging one bit!

We suggest that you decide what is important and where you are willing to compromise. Use Exercise #16 at the back of the book to help you to consider this further.

Compromise is not the same as capitulation, but nor should it be based on a stark refusal to even consider some movement in positions. If you know that you struggle to assert yourself you are likely to fall into one of these entrenched positions. Assertiveness training might be the answer and could well be worth your investment in time and money if it leads to a more fulfilling long-term career.

Top tip

Assertiveness is a complicated topic, but one tip might be of immediate use to you – try never to say 'no' to a potential employer if you can find any way to offer an alternative option to the one being suggested. This can be very effective, not least because you have kept the channels for negotiation open.

How can I find out which careers I am most suited to?

This guide will be helping you not just to decide which career areas suit you but also, as importantly, which type of career might *not* suit you. As you work through the process it can be useful every now and then to find out more about specific job roles so that you can make sure you are searching as positively as possible: www.career-test.co.uk is one of several effective career matching services online and can tell you more about your values, personality and suitability for specific jobs. You should be as truthful as you can when answering the questions in order to gain the most accurate results.

Remember!

When discussing career choices it can be tempting to think only of an ideal world in which you have no restrictions on you at all. This is a productive way to look at your career as you begin to make choices, but it can also be useful to put practical and/or compromise factors into any job search site as this will sometimes throw up careers ideas that you would never have thought of but would suit your circumstances very well.

4.4 Target ... everything

How many CVs do I need?

You should have a master copy of your CV that includes everything relevant to your overall job search. You can then be selective about what information you transfer to your targeted CV, which should be no longer than two A4 pages. This gives you a chance to select just the information that you think your potential employer will be keen to know. There may be no point in telling the law firm you want to work in that you were employed by a high-street shop for six months but it is vital that you inform them of your two weeks' work experience in the legal department of a brokerage firm. Try to keep all of your CVs up to date so that you can send these off quickly should you need to, and see Step Six for more help on creating and maintaining your CV.

What is the 'hidden job market'?

The hidden job market has already been mentioned in earlier sections but we did not always give it this name. This is the job market that the general public do not see; this might be because a vacancy is advertised internally in an organisation, or because a professional is headhunted and so the post is not advertised, or because someone like you has been clever enough to use networking effectively to secure a job before it has been advertised. It is not uncommon for a career opportunity to arise as a result of discussions on cold or warm calls: plenty of people will actually fill out the job application after they have secured a newly created position. A targeted approach is key here – taking control by knowing where you want to be and pushing until you get there.

Jobs within an organisation may be offered to those already working there as internal transfers rather than being advertised widely. This does not necessarily mean that you cannot get in on this if you are outside the organisation, but it does mean that you will need to use your network to find out about such job opportunities and put your name forward. If you are already working in an organisation, you will have access to the intranet, noticeboards and email alerts about internal opportunities. You may also find out about these from colleagues and your manager. If you are already in work when you are starting to research the career market, do take the chance to look at what is going on in your own organisation.

How can I get into the hidden job market?

Talk to people. (Refer to page 92 for network building.) You may have trawled through every job website you can find, you could have spent days looking through adverts, and still the organisations you are looking at will not know you exist. People employ people, not certificates and paperwork. So, talk with the people in your networks who you feel could help you get a foot in the door, and call up or go into the organisations you would like to work for and ask for a job. Yes, it is as simple as that. You will often create more impact if you communicate with people face to face or by telephone. We have had students and clients who were given jobs that were not publicly advertised because they walked into an organisation, got chatting with the frontline staff, and were handed an opportunity to apply there and then.

How can walking help?

This may seem like an odd question but trust us, walking can help you. Or any physical activity that allows you time and space to think and physically move away from the challenge, whether that is job hunting, working out your compromises, or deciding which job to take. In our discussion on the hidden job market we have urged you to walk into company offices and cold call for a job, but here we are talking simply about taking a break. You can become unfocused and so be less targeted in your efforts if you do not pace yourself as you continue on your career journey.

Problems are like people: the further you move away from them, the smaller they seem to get. All of us can become caught up in the minutiae of a difficult task we are doing and lose sight of the bigger picture. By moving away from this, we can gain a better perspective and make sounder judgements overall. It is very similar to buying a house or a car in the sense that we look at so many that we lose sight of what we actually want and what is important to us.

The whole principle of marketing and advertising is that we want something we perceive to be 'better' and that will therefore make us a 'better' person. However, we can tell you (from the little we know) that you are a dedicated, thoughtful and dynamic person. You demonstrated these qualities when you picked up this book and decided to be proactive about your career search. So, when you have been researching the career market for a career in science and you have started to be tempted by jobs in marketing, go for a walk and remind yourself why you are so suitable for a science-related job. Once you have reaffirmed the type of career you want, stop thinking about it and allow your brain to relax before returning to your career market research. After all, your brain has been working hard sifting through potential options for you and deserves a break!

4.5 Making mistakes ... and learning from them

What if I apply and then change my mind?

If you apply, get accepted for an interview but then get a better offer, you should contact the organisation as soon as possible. If it is likely that you may want to work with or for this company in the future, then it is best to be truthful about the new opportunity you are taking. This way you will not offend those potential employers and they will appreciate that you have let them know you are no longer available to work for them.

On the other hand, if you have applied for a job and then you become unsure about whether you would actually like to do the job or not, wait. You may find that an invitation to interview turns up and that through the interview you come to realise that it is a job role you would be able to do well, one you would enjoy and would offer you the chance to move into a more desirable role in the future. You are likely to find that you will do well at interview because you are not too bothered about whether you get the job or not and you can consider it a practice interview. You should always try to get feedback from your interviews if you can.

What if I make a mistake in an interview?

Human error does not prove that you often make mistakes, it proves that you are human. If you have accidently called your interviewer by the wrong name and you realise, then apologise and correct yourself. This rule goes for most errors in an interview, as by correcting yourself you have acknowledged the mistake and then had the confidence and ability to correct it. If you have made a mistake and do not realise this until after the interview, then there is not a lot you can or indeed should do. In some circumstances you may want to contact your interviewer, such as if you have given them the wrong paperwork or details. However, after the event it is very tricky to go back and re-do something, so it can be a wise choice to leave this and try not to worry over it.

Success checklist

✓ Ask yourself if you can change or correct the mistake.
✓ Ask yourself if it will be worth it or whether it will simply highlight the error.
✓ Change it or leave it.
✓ Move on.

What if I am not offered the job after an interview?

You should use this as a chance to learn more about yourself and how to improve your interview technique. Seek feedback from your interviewer(s) but do bear in mind that many organisations may not give this or will take an extremely long time to get back to you; they are busy and have probably seen many applicants and so you might only get a small amount of feedback after a considerable wait. Do not pause your job search while you are awaiting feedback.

While you are waiting for feedback from your interview, take the opportunity to reflect on how you felt it went. Use Exercise #17 at the back of the book to help you focus your thoughts.

This exercise will help you concentrate on how well the interview actually went, as there is quite often a temptation to tell everyone who will listen that it was dreadful or awful and so you will lose your perspective on the event. The word 'dreadful' may well be absolutely the correct word to describe your experience: you were full of dread. Equally, you could well have been full of awe. This does not mean that the result of the interview will be bad, it simply means that your anxiety over the situation has now really flooded in.

Some of us will do very well under pressure, but once that pressurised situation is over we will feel exhausted and start questioning how well things really went. It is best to wait until the stress hormone that has been racing around your body since before your interview has dissipated before you try to judge your interview performance. By using questions in Exercise #17 you will be able to focus on particular parts of it that were under your control, and so if these went badly you will immediately know that *you can* improve next time.

Notice that we have not mentioned here 'failing' at interview, as this suggests that an interview is a test with a simple pass or fail result. If you are not offered a job as a result of any interview then you can often class this as a success despite the disappointing outcome. If you were not the most suitable person for the role, this is your prompt to make yourself more suitable in the future; if you were deemed to be really very unsuited to the role, this is information you need to prompt you to re-examine your plans; if you were narrowly behind another candidate, the phone call to ask for feedback can (surprisingly often) be the moment at which you learn that the other person did not take up the position, and you are still in with a good chance of securing your dream job.

What if I miss the deadline date for an application?

Missing an application deadline does not bode well, as you will have proved that you cannot work to a deadline which is essential in any job. If you have missed it for a very good reason, for example you were in hospital or at a funeral, you could try to appeal to the organisation. However, if you have missed it because you forgot, we recommend that you do not share this with your prospective employer.

Sometimes a deadline is missed because we were waiting on other people. Before you miss the deadline, contact the person who has set the deadline and explain that you expect that you will need an extension due to waiting on other people (references). By doing this you have shown that you are capable of working to a deadline (even if you miss it) and able to judge when more time is required; you have also proved that you have good communication skills and can take the initiative when necessary. If you have to do this, make sure that you keep them apprised of the developing situation and it may be that they offer to interview you without your references at that time.

If you miss a deadline because you have only just seen an advert for a job and you still want to apply for it, contact the organisation and explain that you have only just seen their job opening and ask whether it is still possible to apply. Sometimes you will find that they will still let you apply because they essentially want the right person for the role. Organisations will often set deadlines on their vacancies so that they can collate all the information they need in preparation for the interview process and there is then a time gap which you may be able to exploit. Sometimes a company finds that it has only a few candidates for a position and none of them look promising and so you would be welcome to apply after the advertised deadline.

If the deadline was more than a week previously you would be less likely to be able to apply, but it is always worth checking with the organisation in case it failed to appoint.

What if I miss the interview?

Plenty of people miss interviews but if this happens to you, pause for a minute and consider if there is something else going on for you. Do you really want the job? If you were so keen, why did you not try to catch an earlier bus or set several alarm clocks?

Success checklist

To avoid what could be a disaster follow the list below.

✓ Make sure that you know where the interview is being held (it will not necessarily take place at the office location you expect – there may be a Head Office or local hotel at which the interviews are being conducted).

✓ Plan your timing and journey at least the day before your interview. If you are going to try out the journey, do this at the same time of day as your interview.

✓ Aim to get to your interview 20–30 minutes early to allow yourself time to calm down and let them know that you have arrived.

✓ If you are relying on someone driving you there, check with them when they are picking you up and contact them as soon as they are even a few minutes late.

✓ If you are going by bus, catch an earlier one in case the buses are running late.

✓ Set two alarm clocks to ensure you get up. Even if you do not really need two alarms, this will relax and reassure you.

✓ Try on your interview outfit before the day of your interview so that you can check that it fits, you are not too hot or too cold, and you can move in it easily.

✓ Have a copy of your CV, covering letter, references and any information that you have had from the organisation ready so that you can refer to all of these.

✓ Plan to do something nice after your interview so you can remind yourself that this is just part of a process and that life will go on quite happily after the event.

What if I have just accepted the wrong job?

You have applied for every job you thought might suit you, you have been invited to numerous interviews and have gone back to a handful of second interviews, and you have now been offered a job. You are so delighted that you have said 'Yes!' before you have engaged your brain to triple check that you still want it. Later that week, or even later that day, you start to wonder: 'Do I want to do this job?'

If, on reflection, you believe you might have accepted the wrong job, Exercise #18 will help.

When informing your would-be employer that you made the wrong decision, you should be careful about your wording. Be very specific about why you do not want that particular job and focus on the job role rather than the organisation. We have given you an example below so that you can see how to do this effectively:

I'm sorry but I've now realised that the job is not going to suit me. I should not have accepted it; however, I was so impressed by the organisation and the work culture fostered there that I convinced myself that this was the job for me. On reflection, although I would love to work for your organisation, I do not think that I would be able to commute that far every day.

This example is specific about the feature that has made you feel unable to fulfil the role (commuting) and you have complimented their organisation. They may offer you the chance to work in an office more local to you or allow you to work from home, so you could find you get a more suitable job offer as a result of your focus and honesty.

What if I have started the job and now realise it is not suitable for me?

It is far easier to move a ship on the ocean than to move a ship in port. That is to say, once you are in the job you will have far more opportunities to make it into the job you want. Your first task is to analyse what it is about the job that is 'wrong'. Use Exercise #19 at the back of the book to access help with doing this.

4.6 Managing the process

More than any other step in this guide, Step Four will have demonstrated what an emotional experience your career journey can be. We are asking you to juggle highly demanding tasks (such as cold calling) with very detailed levels of research (so that you can target your efforts); simultaneously we are sharing with you our knowledge of the hidden job market (the very idea of which can be frustrating) and talking you through how best to handle the mistakes you might make along the way.

We know that this is going to be demanding, at times irritating and demoralising, and at other times exciting and almost unbearably nerve wracking. Managing the process is therefore not so much about what you do as how you manage this emotion. If being highly organised helps you feel in control, buy some plastic wallets and highlighter pens and codify the paperwork; if talking helps you work out what you really think and feel, use your support networks heavily at this stage; if you need an energy boost to keep you going, take regular walks to maintain your focus.

Learning how to manage this part of the process is undoubtedly going to pay dividends in the long term. You will find that the tools and techniques you develop now will be there for you to return to again and again throughout your working life – what makes an excellent candidate for a job is very similar to what makes an excellent professional once appointed.

Further reading

As part of managing the process, you may find it useful to do further research using these recommended websites:

4.2 Deciphering the career market

Finding out more about different types of careers:

https://nationalcareersservice.direct.gov.uk/advice/planning/jobfamily/Pages/default.aspx – This has a huge range of job profiles for you to peruse.

www.ed.ac.uk/schools-departments/careers/using-careers-service/cvs-apps-interviews/business-awareness/finding-about-careers – This website gives you more detailed information about different careers, including 'day in the life of … ' diary entries from graduates of the university.

4.3 Some practicalities to consider

Finding out which career suits you:

www.career-test.co.uk – This website takes you to a quiz to test which of your personality traits will be useful in the world of work.

www.bbc.co.uk/science/humanbody/mind/surveys/careers – This website takes you through another quiz to help you pinpoint which type of career will most suit you.

www.simplypsychology.org/learning-kolb.html – This link takes you to see an image of Kolb's experiential cycle and gives you some more useful information about it. It will help you to understand the ways you work best.

Find out more about cold calling:

www.businessballs.com/cold_calling.htm – This explains what cold calling is and gives you some techniques to help you do this successfully.

4.4 Target … everything

Advice about how to enter the 'hidden job market':

www.forbes.com/sites/nextavenue/2013/08/12/6-ways-to-crack-the-hidden-job-market – This article gives you advice about how to access the hidden job market.

www.birmingham.ac.uk/alumni/careers/graduatecareers/applying/hiddenjobmarket.aspx – This article explains how to access the hidden job market.

4.5 Making mistakes … and learning from them

Advice about interview mistakes:

http://career-advice.monster.com/job-interview/interview-preparation/avoid-common-interview-mistakes/article.aspx – This offers advice about the top interview mistakes and how to remedy them.

Step Five: First approaches

Read this section now if:

- You have yet to think about networking and how to do it.
- You are not sure that you have a professional network.
- You want to make the most of the networks you have.
- You are working outside your home country and so feel separated from your usual support network.
- You have never heard of personal branding.
- You are not sure you like the idea of personal branding.
- You want to make the most of your personal branding.
- You are not clear on what a placement or internship is, or what the differences between these might be.
- You are trying to decide whether to undertake a placement or internship.
- You want to make the most of the internship or placement you have done.

5.1 Introduction: why does it matter?

Funnily enough, many first approaches matter rather less as a way to make an initial move towards a great career, and rather more as a way to ensure that you do not place any obstacles in your own way at a later stage of the process. Having an enticing social media profile, for example, is going to be something you achieve as a first move, but it will not become relevant unless an employer at a later stage looks you up online. Personal branding has to be perfected now, but again you might not need to rely on it until later.

Placements or internships are often a first move in a career strategy, and they have their place there, but they will become valuable again later when you come to prove your worth to an employer at interview, for example, or once you have joined an organisation.

Our point is that we are calling these first approaches because you will do them now, before you face other aspects of the process, but they will be of continuing benefit to you for many months and years to come, and will need to be refreshed and renewed as your professional life develops. Too often we have seen people assume that answering an advert or attending a careers fair is the first move in their career plans, with no idea that they have lost the job already because an internet search of their name brings up a wildly inappropriate image of them in Ibiza three years ago; a stage of life from which you might think you have progressed can haunt you for decades unless you make your first moves, first.

5.2 Making contact: building your networks

What sort of networks should I have?

It can help you hugely if you are able to identify the separate networks you might have. All of us rely on different groups of people to help and support us in our lives and our careers. Sometimes a person might fit into several of our networks, or fulfil several roles in one network. By identifying your networks and the roles fulfilled by people in those networks, you will be able to make the best possible use of them.

We will offer you here a list of possible networks that you might want to cultivate, with some of the ways that the people in each network might help you in your career plans. You can then add to the list of networks and ways in which members of each can help you, so that you create a network list that is exclusive to your situation and needs. Do not worry at this stage if you cannot think of anyone to include in each network – that will come later as you follow our advice about expanding and maintaining your networks.

Network 1: Close and supportive network

This network could include:

- Your immediate or close family.
- Close personal friends (but not necessarily 'work friends').
- Counsellors, mentors or similar close advisors and supporters – those most interested in you as a person rather than you as a professional.

These network contacts will be able to:

- Offer you support regardless of how well or badly things are going.
- Pick you up if things go wrong.
- Boost your confidence as you work towards your perfect career.
- Be honest with you about who you are and what you are trying to achieve.

You need this network because:

- It offers emotional support when times get tough.
- It reminds you that you are going to succeed, and that you deserve that success.

Remember!

These networks are there to help you. Before you move on, look again at what these people are expected to do in this network. If the people you have in mind are not able to fulfil these roles, then move them to another network. If, for example, you have a close relative who is well connected but especially critical of you and what you are hoping to achieve, move that relative firmly out of this network and into your 'professional contacts network'. This is a good way to ensure that you feel in control of your networks and make them work for you rather than against you.

Network 2: Endorsement network

This network could include:

- Teachers, tutors, study skills advisors, mentors, managers and colleagues.
- You will notice already that some people (such as mentors) will sit within several of your networks. This is as it should be, as one person might be able to help you in several different ways. If you had a close relative who also employed you at some point, then that person might sit within networks 1, 2, 3 and 4.

These network contacts will be able to:

- Be referees (remember that a colleague can offer you an employment reference – it does not always have to be a manager who does this).
- Help you plan the next step forward in terms of your skills development.
- Keep their eyes open and recommend you to potential employers.

You need this network because:

- If you have a pool of potential referees in your mind already, this makes it easier to pick the perfect person to give you a reference for a particular job.

- If you are actively working with this network, your referees will be ready to look at a job description and your application form and produce the best possible reference for you.
- Although we all need encouragement, it also helps to have practical advice about how we can maximise our chances of success.
- Being recommended to an organisation can be the easiest way to get a job.
- By identifying the members of this network you can make sure that your situation is clear in their minds; that way they will be ready to mention your name as soon they hear of an opportunity.

Network 3: Professional contacts network

This network could include:

- Any of your present or previous employers (and/or colleagues).
- Anyone you have met in a formal careers setting, such as a careers or recruitment fair.
- Anyone you have met as a result of a placement or internship.
- Any contact you have available to you as a result of professional activity (such as the contact details you took from a noticeboard or organisational intranet whilst on placement).
- Professionals you have talked to about a vacancy, even if you did not pursue the job in the end.
- Recruitment agencies.

These network contacts will be able to:

- Tell you about vacancies that are coming up.
- Keep you informed about developments in your target organisations.
- Advise you on how your target sector or sectors are developing.

You need this network because:

- It is a quick way to get the information you need.
- You do not always know what you need to know until someone tells you: this group of people might be proactive in telling you what is happening so that you can use this to your advantage.
- This could be the best way to find out about opportunities that are not yet being advertised, giving you a huge advantage over other potential applicants.

Network 4: Personal and professional development network

This network could include:

- Careers advisors.
- Coaches and mentors.

- Managers.
- Professional bodies.

These network contacts will be able to:

- Ensure that you keep your skills, qualifications and registrations up to date.
- Save you time and money by advising you on the best training courses to attend.
- Help you present yourself to the careers market in the best way.

You need this network because:

- It is easy to panic and take a wrong turn, leaving you on a training course that is time consuming and costly, when there might be a better course out there.
- Often it is not more training you need, you simply need to present your existing qualifications and experience in the best way – these network supporters can help with that.
- Enhancing your interview skills, psychometric test practice, CV checking – all of these will help you move ahead and are offered by this group.

Top tip

We are seeing increasing numbers of mature students (particularly in further education) entering into an apprenticeship to get the benefits of formal training and practical experience. With a job market that is always fluctuating, this is sometimes the most sensible way to begin a new career. The drawbacks of an apprenticeship are that you may be on a low income during your training and there are no guarantees that you will be offered a permanent position once you have completed that training in an organisation. However, you will come out with skills and experience to put on your CV and you will also be able to build an impressive professional development network whilst you are training.

Network 5: Miscellaneous network

This network could include:

- Anyone you feel could help you but who does not seem to fit easily into any of the other networks.

These network contacts will be able to:

- Help you in ways you have not yet considered. They may not be of obvious benefit to you today, but old friends can find themselves in a professional position to help you, managers change jobs and need new staff, old contacts can become useful referees when you change your career plans.

- Keep you in mind and introduce you to new contacts who might fit perfectly into one of your networks.

You need this network because:

- You will not want to discard anyone from your networks just because you cannot find an immediate reason to include them.
- Your plans can change and your network needs might change with them.
- Other people's lives change and that could change their professional profile.

Remember!

Networks need not be local – keep in touch with international contacts as regularly as you do with your local contacts.

Now that you have a basic list of networks, think about what else each of these might do for you in your specific situation, and note down also any other networks that you could usefully create for yourself.

Who might be in my networks?

It is sometimes said that the most successful professionals are those with the largest address books and there is some truth in that. The first rule is not to leave anyone out of your networks, so use your miscellaneous network to include anyone who might be of value to you in the future, but who does not have an obvious place in a network now.

To populate your networks in the first instance, go to multiple sources.

Success checklist

- ✓ Your email address book.
- ✓ Any business cards you have collected.
- ✓ Your current work colleagues, if you have any.
- ✓ Past work colleagues, if you have any.
- ✓ Contacts from previous voluntary work.
- ✓ Contacts from any challenges or team activities you have undertaken.
- ✓ Your family and friends.
- ✓ Friends from specific areas – school, college, social groups and so on.

For each of these source areas, try to capture the details of every possible useful contact you already have. Remember that this is a way to move forward in your career, so try to see even family and friends as potential business contacts. Now is the time to check on the professional standing of each of your more distant relatives – more often than you might expect, this sort of searching can bring up useful contacts you never realised you had.

Top tip

If you can, keep details of two ways to contact each person (an email address and a mobile, or two different phone numbers). That way, you can still get hold of them even if they change jobs or relocate.

How do I build up a network?

Once you have your existing contacts slotted into your networks by following the success checklist, you will need to consider which of your networks needs to be extended. Most people will realise at this point that they are a little low on contacts in at least one area. Perhaps you do not have more than a couple of people to offer you references, or you are not able to keep up to date with professional developments in your chosen area. Whatever lack you identify, Exercise #20 at the back of the book will help.

Careful!

We will be discussing social media networking with you when we come to look at personal branding, but beware of believing that social media sites such as LinkedIn™ can do all of the work for you. This is a useful site for keeping you in touch with people, and advertising likely jobs to you, but there are plenty of 'LinkedIn collectors' out there, people who just like to have the longest possible list of LinkedIn contacts without actually keeping in touch with or using those contacts very much. This is called 'passive networking', and it has its place, but you also need to be networking more actively, as we are suggesting in this chapter.

Here are two websites that you might find useful when trying to establish your networks:

www.bni.co.uk – a global networking organisation with local groups that you can join. They also offer training and meetings to help you network and gain more business.

www.findnetworkingevents.com – a useful website that will help you find local networking events that are taking place.

How do I make best use of my networks?

Little and often, and with precision. Each time you face a hurdle (I need a reference, I feel low, I am not sure how to upskill, I cannot seem to see openings in my area), then turn to your networks first. Be clear about what you need from your contact at that moment and ask for just what you need. That might not be a lengthy email exchange or a meeting; it could equally usefully be passing on another contact to you, or sending you to the right website. If you are specific about your needs and clear that you will not waste their time, contacts will feel honoured to be asked and pleased to help you.

How do I maintain my networks?

This is one of the most demanding aspects of networking, not because it is difficult to do but because it takes constant care. Exercise #21 at the back of the book will help.

Should I name-drop?

Yes. 'Name-dropping' means mentioning a contact's name in conversation or at interview in order to impress someone. That is one of the purposes of a network, so do not be coy here; if you are sure that mentioning a name will impress, use it.

When can I close down my networks?

Never. Once you have secured the position you want, keep a light touch maintenance of your networks going so that you remain alert to the next opportunity, or ways to maximise your current position.

What is a mentor and should I get one?

A professional mentor is someone who has gone down a similar path before you and can give you advice to help with all aspects of your professional life. You might also have educational mentors or personal mentors. A mentor shares wisdom with you and encourages you. Some famously successful people have had or still do have mentors: Bill Gates, Tiger Woods, Elizabeth Taylor, Dr Martin Luther King, Barack Obama, Heath Ledger, Meryl Streep. The list goes on. So, why would you need a mentor? Well, we have all experienced that frustrating moment when we have exhausted our own motivation and the problem that seemed manageable last week has grown beyond all recognition. A mentor can see the bigger picture and come up with solutions, even if it is simply to help us reduce the problem to bite-sized chunks. A professional athlete such as the tennis player Andy Murray would not expect to turn up on court without his coach/mentor. That designated person is the one who will give him advice from the court side, cheer him on, and give him that special look that says 'you can do this and what's more, you will do it. I believe in you.'

You may find that you need to pay for a mentor and so you should seek advice from others about who you could go to. If you are just coming out of education, you may ask a lecturer. If you know people within an industry that you want to be working in, ask them if they know of anyone suitable. Your mentor may even be a family member but be warned that this may cause disruption in your personal relationship.

Top tip

Ask around and only choose a mentor who has succeeded in the area in which you are hoping to develop. There is no use in appealing for help to somebody who has yet to tread the path you wish to follow.

5.3 Personal branding

What is personal branding?

Personal branding is the way you present yourself to the professional world. This will differ in some significant ways from the self you show to family and friends, or your current work or study colleagues. It can involve how you dress, how you present material to others, how you craft an image of yourself on social media, and even – for some people – how you talk. In this section our focus is on your online and real presence as it relates to making a career move.

How do I clean up my real life brand?

Your real life brand, in this context, is any means by which you are in contact with a potential employer. This could be at a distance (a CV or application form) or face to face (at a recruitment/careers fair, professional event or interview). Follow each step on the checklist below to ensure that you have this covered.

Success checklist

✓ Do the research – it is only by knowing what an organisation is looking for that you can decide which side of yourself you want to offer for inspection. Target every single document you produce to the demands of a role or an organisation.

✓ Work your benefits – by working through the application process as we suggest in the next step, you will be able to identify clear benefits that you have brought to a previous employer, and/or could bring to this employer. Keep these firmly in mind as they are now part of your brand.

✓ Sit alongside the employer – that is, make sure that you seem the 'right sort of person' for the role. You will not want to radically change who you are, and you would not apply for a job that required this of you, but if you are asked to dress casually, or have an informal job chat on the phone, these might be hints that they are looking for a less formal team player than you might have expected.

(Continued)

Careful!

You can choose to dress rather more casually as a result of their suggestions, and you might want to come across as friendly and approachable in a casual, pre-interview job chat, but do not be fooled – you still need to be meticulous in your research and ready to present yourself as well informed and well equipped to do the job.

(Continued)

✓ Keep control – your written forms of personal branding are going to be crucial, so make sure that you know exactly where your CV is and what it looks like. Do not let a recruitment agency take control of your CV without your knowledge so that you turn up to interview with a CV that is branded to the agency rather than to you. You will want to target your CV and application to each particular organisation and vacancy, so make sure that you have a copy of the CV and application beside you as you prepare for interview.

✓ Take your time – the danger of working hard to present a sense of yourself that is true, but not the complete, unvarnished truth of how your family or close friends would see you, is that you can let the branding slip. If you are asked an unexpected question, either at interview or in a less formal setting, take a moment to collect your thoughts before you answer.

✓ Be confident about what you are doing. You have done your research, you know that you have what it takes to do the job – now all you have to do is show the sides of your experience, skills set and personality that prove this.

Remember!

Personal branding is not about lying, it is about demonstrating that you are the right person for a job. We all have multifaceted personalities and yet we are not selling an organisation the self that slumps on the sofa in the evening, or who loves to dance the night away each weekend. These are still important parts of you, but not the parts that will sell you to an employer when first you meet.

How do I clean up my virtual brand?

Your virtual brand is the image of yourself that exists online and in the media. To clean it up you need persistence. Use several different search engines to find yourself online regularly, to check that what is out there is the 'you' that you want the professional world to see. Less-professional-looking images can be protected by passwords.

Top tip

If you are starting to feel that online branding is going to compromise the fun of your social networking, remember that you can always set up a social media page with a slightly different version of your name so that it is less easy to track. Be bold about asking friends for their help with your online presence. If you are tagged on several photos in which you do not appear at your best, ask them to untag you or remove the photos for a while.

How do I use my branding when networking?

For your online brand this can largely be minor maintenance, once you have done the groundwork. Knowing that you have cleaned up your virtual brand is only half the battle at the outset – you now need to boost your professional brand online. This could involve creating a blog that reflects your interests and posting to it regularly. It might mean writing on other blogs that have a link to your personal or professional interests. You might also think about tweeting from any conference you are attending, or ensuring that the newspaper write-up of an event in which you were involved actually names you specifically. Once you have done this work you can feel satisfied that an online search for you will do more than just show a clean brand – it will show evidence of an upbeat, engaged and informed professional.

You could create a webpage for your extended CV with examples, pictures and short film clips about projects you have worked on and experiences you have gained. Your university, college or place of work might be able to help you with this and it could offer you a long-term online presence that could be of value for many years.

In talking about your virtual brand we have been considering your online presence, but your networks are also representing a virtual brand. If any of your contacts are likely to recommend you, or if you ask for a reference, it is your job to guarantee that the network contact has the most up-to-date information about you, and knows enough about the context to give you the best possible recommendation or reference.

For your real-life brand you will feel more in control, principally because you will be offering information in a well-defined situation such as an interview. You now need to keep control as much as you can, and that means preparing well in advance. If the organisation is asking for an affable and hardworking team player who is keen to accept new challenges, then you can reflect this in your brand. Make sure that you demonstrate these qualities, if you can, in your presentation, or prepare examples that you can use at interview to support the brand you are trying to portray.

> ### Remember!
>
> As with so much else in building a career, this is really all about research. If you are clear about what is needed and confident that you can deliver, everything will come more easily.

How friendly should my brand be?

Having an effective brand does not mean seeming unapproachable or aloof. It would look rather strange if the only material that appeared about you online, for example, were professionally focused. It would be like refusing to sit down at an interview because you were so eager to appear formal and professional. Once you have cleaned up your brand and then boosted it online, and as you produce each new set of documentation or prepare each interview presentation, ask someone from your close and supportive and/or your endorsement network to check that you are giving the impression of being professional and yet not too aloof or off-putting.

How much should I try to stand out?

We would urge you only to stand out in response to your research. Producing a CV in green ink, or appearing in tangerine trousers and pink hair on every one of your online photos, can seem to you to be a way to differentiate yourself from everyone else, and it will indeed make you a little more distinctive, but you need to be absolutely sure that this is seen as positive by everyone, and this is not likely to be the case. Of course, you might say that you would not work for anyone who does not like your personal style of branding, and that is reasonable as long as you are making a conscious decision to approach your career in this way. If not, work on standing out professionally rather than letting your personality shine through to the detriment of everything else.

5.4 Placements and internships

What is a placement/internship?

The terms 'placement' and 'internship' can cause confusion as they tend to be used interchangeably to describe a period of activity in an organisation that is not your own. For college and university students this could be a period of work experience, for those looking to get into a career it could be quite an extended time working within an organisation but without a contract of employment (although an internship agreement could be in place). For some students a placement might be an academic placement, where a student works in an organisation but might be working solely on a research project of some sort, or it might be a combination of day-to-day work and research. The use of these terms also varies across borders. So, depending on the country within which you are living and the situation within which you are working, you might believe yourself to be on either a placement or an internship; for the purposes of this section we are going to use the term 'placement' to cover all of these activities and opportunities.

How do I get a placement?

Very often placements are provided for students or are an automatic part of a job, giving employees the chance to experience different aspects of the workplace. This can make your life easier, but it can also potentially be restrictive. Always explore the possibility of creating your own placement, with the support of your college, university or employer. Not only might this help you to stand out from others, it could also ensure you undertake a placement that is uniquely useful to you, your interests and your aims.

What would I do on a placement?

This should always be negotiated well in advance of actually going on the placement. You will want to offer value to the placement provider, but you will also need to gain from the experience, so make sure that both parties are clear about your aims. There are some important questions that you need to ask and have answered before you commit.

Success checklist

✓ What hours will you be expected to work, and is there any flexibility over working hours?

✓ Will you be given a desk and computer from which to work?

✓ What duties will you be expected to fulfil?

✓ Who will be managing you?

✓ How much time will be dedicated to your own research (if you are planning on doing this as part of a placement)?

✓ How much access will you be given to the organisation's material, if you are carrying out a research project of some sort?

✓ Will you be expected to present your findings, or share your experience, in a presentation or report produced for the placement provider?

Would I be paid for a placement?

Not unless you have negotiated pay in advance. This is clearly going to be crucial when you come to make a decision about whether to undertake a particular placement. It must work for you, and you need to feel confident that what you will gain will be worth the investment of your time.

Careful!

Not being paid may also mean not being offered travel expenses. This could be a severe obstacle, especially if you will have to pay hundreds of pounds and spend many hours travelling to and from your placement. It might be possible to arrange off-peak working hours to reduce the costs, so negotiate fully in advance.

What can I expect to gain from a placement?

This will depend to a large degree on what you plan to gain from it. You need to work out, before you go on the placement, what you aim to achieve; that way you will be ready to make the best possible use of your time. You might already know why you want to undertake a placement, but if you are less than clear, the following checklist of possible reasons could help.

Checklist

- To find out more about a career area.
- To decide whether you like a career.
- To network with professionals in an area relevant to your future plans.
- To gain some experience.
- To expand your portfolio of material to share with future employers.
- To create some engaging 'war stories' (see page 20) for interview.
- To show an organisation that you are worth employing at the end of the placement.
- To prove your worth to other future employers.
- To get used to the rhythm and demands of the workplace.
- To carry out a research project as part of an academic placement linked to a course of study.
- To gain some free career development training.
- To develop the specific skills you know you need that are not on your current CV.
- To work out the right level of entry for you in an area of the career market.

Remember!

What you are asked to do on placement need not deter you from the goal upon which you decided before you arrived. If you are firm in your resolve you will be able to suit your purposes alongside any other activities that take place.

How can I make the most of a placement?

It is only natural that your focus will be on the experience of the placement itself, how to get there, what it will be like, and the sort of people you might meet, but the benefits of any placement will be greatly increased if you prepare well in advance. Go to Exercise #22 to help you structure your thoughts about your placement.

Top tips

Never see the work you put into securing a placement as a waste of time. If a placement provider has already filled the place, ask if you can be considered for future placement opportunities. Contact multiple providers at the same time – you can always turn some of these into a straight work experience rather than a more in-depth placement. No contact you make is a wasted contact.

What six things should I do before going on a placement?

Success checklist

✓ Negotiate the practicalities (do you need flexi-hours, or a day off at any point? Where exactly is the placement activity to take place?).

✓ Check your working space (will you have a desk? Will you need to take your own laptop?).

✓ Share any minor anxieties you have either with someone who has been there on placement before, or someone alongside whom you will be working; small, practical points such as the dress code, or whether there is a canteen, can be distracting as you prepare for a placement.

✓ Print out and keep beside you the records you produced in the exercises and check-lists above; add to these the results of an internet search on the organisation. Showing that you care enough to have researched a placement provider thoroughly is always impressive; it also offers you some useful conversation topics on the first day.

✓ Change your status on social media to show where and when you are on placement (as long as your placement provider is happy for you to do this) – let the world know how you are developing your career potential.

✓ Make sure that you know how to keep in touch with your tutor or professional mentor during your placement – especially if it is over a traditional holiday time.

What six things should I do before completing a placement?

Success checklist

✓ Plan out your report/reflection on the placement, if you are not expected to produce some written work as a result of it. Even if there is no formal reporting, keeping a log of your activities and reflections will be useful for your skills and experience inventories.

✓ Make as many contacts as you can, with a note of their contact details – this will boost your professional contacts network. (Refer to page 92 for network building.)

✓ Check every noticeboard (both real life and on the organisation's intranet) you can find to make sure you are aware of positions that might become available, or develop-ments in the organisation that might be of interest to you in the future.

✓ Try to arrange to go back to the organisation for further placements or part-time work, or apply for any vacancies you have found.

✓ If you are to report on the experience, take away with you (with permission, of course) any material you might need, such as headed paper, or company brochures and reports.

✓ Print off any emails that might be useful in future, either because you will use them (with permission) as references in a report, or because you think you might need a reminder in future of contact details and records of useful professional conversations.

Placements are such a valuable way to introduce yourself to the career market that even if these are not a traditional part of your course of study or way of working, it is a good idea to think about undertaking a placement as part of your career strategy. Even if you are in work, negotiating a short placement elsewhere is often possible, either in your current or a target organisation. There is controversy every now and again about how much placements and internships might exploit those undertaking them, and you will want to avoid this happening to you. The best way to do this is to prepare well in advance and be focused on what you need to achieve – this section will have helped you do that.

5.5 Managing the process

We hope that by the end of this step, you are fired up ready to make your bold moves towards becoming well known in the career market. You should remember to be clear about what it is you are striving for and how you are going to get it. There is nothing better than a well-considered plan that has helped you succeed in your goals. A few things you should remember: think international (your employer is!), know the purpose of your actions, work on each plan little and often to keep it moving, use everyone you know but ensure that you are clear about the purpose they serve, and most importantly remember that if you do not ask, you do not get.

Further reading

As part of managing the process, you may find it useful to do further research using the recommended websites listed below.

5.2 Making contact: building your network

Networking organisations and events:

www.bni.co.uk – This is a useful website for finding networks that you might want to join.
www.findnetworkingevents.com – This helps you find networking events in your local area, which will then help you build your professional profile.

5.3 Personal branding

Advice about building a personal brand:

www.forbes.com/sites/shamahyder/2014/08/18/7-things-you-can-do-to-build-an-awesome-personal-brand – This website looks at what personal branding is and how to go about doing this.

https://gb.linkedin.com – This is a very popular site for those building a professional profile and networking using the internet.

5.4 Placements and internships

Advice about how to make the most of your work placement or internship:

www.birmingham.ac.uk/generic/internships/documents/making-the-most.pdf – This is an article on the University of Birmingham website about how to make the most of your placement or internship.

www.pwc.com/us/en/careers/campus/internships/make-the-most-of-your-internship.jhtml – This also gives you tips about how to make the most of your internship.

www.jobs.ac.uk/careers-advice/careers-advice/2223/making-the-most-of-an-internship – This website gives you even more tips about how to make the most of your internship.

Step Six: Making your move

Read this section now if:

- You feel confident about the roles you want to apply for and want to start work on a CV so as to be ready to go.
- You have just one CV and want to be more targeted in your approach.
- You have heard of a covering letter or email and do not really know how to produce one.
- You are faced with a blank application form and you have no idea where to start.
- Online application forms scare you.
- You believe you have the skills and qualities needed in a role but struggle to express yourself.
- You want to be able to prove conclusively that you are the person for a job.

6.1 Introduction: why does it matter?

This is the last part of the selection process that is going to be private and totally under your control. It will set you up for all that is to happen between here and your successful appointment, so it is a crucial stepping stone along your journey. The reason privacy matters is that it gives you the space to consider, without any great pressure, exactly how you want to represent yourself, the person you want to be as you approach the next challenge. There are guidelines for CVs, but no absolute rules; there are boxes to fill out in an application form, but no-one dictating how you must divide the material between the boxes; covering letters need to be effective, but the material you include in them is up to you.

This level of freedom can, of course, be daunting when you first come to think about it, but it does give you the chance to craft at least some of your interview (they are bound to ask you about something on your CV) and take some control over the selection process as a whole (you can spend as long as you need to work through an application form and decide which facets of yourself you want to foreground).

Knowing that this is so important, but also that it is a challenge, we are aiming in this step to give you succinct and practical answers to questions that we hear time and time again. This will not be an overview of every aspect of CV writing or completing an application form – without us standing beside you this is impossible – but we believe that it will be a safe guiding hand helping you through the journey.

6.2 Your CV (Curriculum Vitae)

Should I go for an online or paper CV?

You will need both. Even if you are only planning to submit CVs online, it helps to see this in hard copy form so that you can proofread it and check that the layout is exactly as you want it to be. Attached to an email or sent via an e-portal there is no guarantee that the layout will remain exactly the same, but you will know that it left you in as impressive a state as you could make it.

Remember!

Your CV is about giving you some control, and that is why you will need to keep a copy near to hand during telephone interviews and also keep a copy on you when you go to a face-to-face interview. It will remind you of just how you have presented yourself to each potential employer.

How long should my CV be?

Two sides of an A4 sheet are standard, so unless you know that in your target industry it is the norm to produce more or less than that, stick to this guide. Less than two pages might suggest that you have nothing much to offer; more than two pages proves that you cannot be concise about what you would bring to the organisation.

> **Remember!**
>
> Your CV is your sales pitch; it is made by you, to sell you in the career marketplace. It has to get you to interview – that is its principal purpose. With this in mind, many CV decisions become easy.

Should I have an expert prepare my CV?

Having an expert check over the CV you have prepared can be useful, but need not cost you money. You might ask for help from your Careers Service or an experienced professional such a family member or friend. Do not lose control of your CV. If an expert prepares it from scratch, you might find that you do not feel comfortable being that person at interview. If you are being represented by a recruitment agency you might find yourself with a CV that represents their needs more than yours.

> **Careful!**
>
> One of us once helped out at an interview at which the first question was 'Which of these candidates are you?' Through the complexities of a hard copy CV posted to the organisation, an online CV sent off and a recruitment agency intervention, the interview panel were faced with three CVs for the same person – so insist on keeping a tight rein on how your CV is used.

If I produce a paper CV, what sort of paper should I use?

The best quality you can afford, but stick to white or cream.

Would a coloured font make a good impression?

You should only use a coloured font if you are certain of your target reader's response. Remember that the first read through of CVs might be by a member of Human Resources, or a recruitment consultant, so although green ink and a quirky font might make you stand out in some areas, it may result in your CV being discarded. Make an impression in what you write rather than the font style and you can guarantee to make a good first showing.

Top tip

Fonts matter. Times New Roman is a very traditional font, whereas Arial is often seen as more modern; Calibri is an easy to read font whilst Lucinda Sans can be a little childish in effect. Try putting your CV into different font styles until you find one that you think is easy to read and reflects well on your sales pitch. Avoid the really weird fonts!

Is there a special layout?

The only point to remember about your CV layout is that there is no pre-scribed layout. Make sure that you produce a document that works for what you are trying to achieve: you are just trying to get as far as an interview. So, your CV is not the entire course of your life, as the name suggests, but edited highlights of your professional/educational life so far, with a few brief mentions of activities that are more personal (interests and achievements, for example). You have as much leeway as you need, as long as you can stick to two pages of A4 paper. If you are running out of space, try narrowing the margins. Use bullet-pointed lists where you want to highlight a few points and headings to guide the reader rather than too much prose. In short, keep polishing the CV until your marketable facets shine.

Careful!

However nice the person looking at your CV, he or she is likely to have one key priority: to put as many CVs as possible from the huge pile received into new piles – 'Yes', 'No' and 'Maybe'. This is not said so as to panic you, it is just a fact of selection and you need to be ready to fight to make it to the first pile. Make every word count; make every decision with the same care you would give to any document that could change your life.

Do I have to include my date of birth or National Insurance Number on my CV?

No, not unless you have been specifically asked to do so. If you are working outside your home country you might expect to include details similar to this so as to reassure the employer (it might be a work permit number, a national insurance or tax number or social benefit registration number), but you are not required to do so. As with so much else on a CV, ask yourself the same question – 'will including these details move me a step nearer to success?'

What is a personal profile and should I include it?

This is a short piece of writing, two to three sentences long, at the beginning of your CV. It appears just below your name and contact details and sets out your sales pitch in brief. If you find yourself writing more than three sentences, you are including too much. If you cannot think of a single thing to include in your personal profile, consider again whether the job for which you are applying is one that would really suit you.

> **Careful!**
>
> Although anyone producing a CV will want to make their personal profile as persuasive as possible, it will be difficult to engage your reader if you use clichéd phrases such as 'dynamic team player' and 'results-focused salesperson' – try to make your personal profile truly personal by making it sound genuine and committed to the role you hope to fill.

What headings should I include?

Although we have told you that there are no rules as such, there are conventional headings that you might want to include so that your reader can navigate your CV easily and be impressed by what is included. Look at Exercise #23 at the back of the book to get more information about what should be included under each heading.

What if there are gaps in my CV?

Try producing what is called a 'functional CV'. Rather than listing your jobs in your Career History section, list instead the functions you performed (such as 'Administration', 'Customer Service' or 'Research') and give examples from across the entire range of your career without making specific reference to any one job. You can, if you like, add in a less prominent section entitled 'Employment' in which you could list your jobs in brief, with one or two lines per job. That way the focus is on what you have achieved and the skills you have acquired rather than on any career gaps.

What if I failed an exam?

If you undertook a course that is relevant to your job hopes, you might want to include it even if you did not do very well in, or were unable to take, the final exam. Including 'Undertook a course in French conversation' at least gives an interviewer the chance to ask you about this area of interest.

Can I lie on my CV?

Even if this is not a moral conundrum for you, it might be a practical consideration. If you are distracted at interview by worrying that you might be asked about your lie, you are less likely to perform well. If you begin work and have the lie hanging over you, aware that you could be challenged on this at any time, you are not going to enjoy the job. If the lie is about something significant related to the job, you are also likely to underperform. Added to this, if you are found out in some types of falsehood, your contract of employment might be invalid. With so many good, practical reasons not to lie, it is hard to think of any situations where it would be worth your while.

Do I have to declare any medical condition or disability?

This is a document that is designed to get you as far as an interview, so you will need to make a judgement call here. If you believe that your medical condition or disability will not have any adverse effect on your interview, or your ability (with reasonable adjustments) to do the job, then it would be understandable if you chose not to go into any detail here. A CV says 'I can do this job!' rather than 'Let me tell you all about myself in every respect'. Having said that, some people would feel so uncomfortable at interview if they had not mentioned a medical condition or disability that they would perform far better if they could present the information up front, on their CV. As we have stressed before, this is your CV and so it is your decision.

Remember!

If you fill out an application form (which you might still do, even if you have also submitted a CV) you may well be asked whether any reasonable adjustments need to be made to allow you to undertake the interview. In this case you will need to let the potential employer know if you do need these adjustments to be made, although it is worth noting that members of the interview panel will probably not see this section of the form.

Is one version of my CV enough?

No. Unless you are only applying for one single job, you will need to target your CV according to each opportunity. Instead, create a lengthy 'master CV', and then just edit this down each time you use it so that it is perfectly targeted to the situation.

Should there be an online version of my CV?

There are three options for putting your CV online. The first is to submit an electronic copy of your CV to a recruitment agency and it will be added to its bank of CVs for employers to peruse. We would urge you to check once it is uploaded to ensure that there are no mistakes and that the formatting has not been changed. This allows employers to find you without you doing too much work. The second option is to have a web page just displaying your CV. You can print this web address onto business cards, ready to hand them out. (If you have limited access to a computer and so cannot readily send your CV by email, you could give this web address in case the employer wants to check your CV straightaway.) The third option is that you create your own website. There are many products that allow you quite easily to design a website and this will offer you scope for more than the traditional two-page CV. On your site you can add pictures, film clips and audio files to give your target employer a well-rounded feel of who you are and how you would benefit the company.

Of course, LinkedIn™ and other social media sites may already be giving you a professional online profile to which you can refer employers.

How do I target my CV?

By finding out as much as you can about the organisation to which you are applying and the type of person they would like to employ. There are numerous places you could look for the information you need.

Success checklist

✓ The job advert – if this is being shown online and in hard copy (such as in a newspaper or poster) then check both copies to make sure you have grasped everything.

✓ Other job adverts – if the organisation is recruiting more widely, you might find some revealing little pieces of information in the other job adverts it is putting out (such as plans for expansion, relocation, a change in market).

✓ The job description – this differs from the job outline given in an advert and you will usually have to ask for a copy. A job description gives an overview of the role and its purpose in the organisation, as well as the main duties and responsibilities involved.

(Continued)

(Continued)

✓ The person specification – again, this might be sent to you once you express an interest in the job. Not every job will have a person specification attached to it. A person specification differs from a job description in that it gives a list of 'essential' and 'desirable' skills, knowledge, qualifications, qualities and experience.

✓ The application form – this may be a fairly standard form, but sometimes certain questions will give you useful clues about the type of person they are looking for, or the qualities they value.

✓ The organisation's website – make sure that what you are looking at is the official website of the organisation rather than an umbrella site that simply includes information on your target organisation.

(Continued)

Careful!

At interview make sure that you only refer to aspects of the organisation that you can verify from the company's official site. Other sites might have an agenda that could bend the truth and cause confusion or upset at an interview. You need to demonstrate that you have taken a real interest in the company, but also that you know how to verify online material.

(Continued)

✓ Via an internet search, especially of news channels – if you scroll down past the first ten hits on an internet search for your organisation you are likely to find some other sites (such as review sites, or political campaign sites) which may give you an interesting view from a different perspective. News channels also have excellent internal search engines and so it will be easy for you to pick up any recent breaking news on your organisation.

(Continued)

Remember!

Your target organisation might be owned by a much larger corporation, so make sure that you search as widely as you can and follow the clues that take you to any other related sites.

(Continued)

✓ The job chat – if the advert offers you the chance to talk to someone with whom you will be working in your target organisation, you should make the call. Not only might it give you the chance to mention information that nobody else has acquired, it also means that – if the organisation is logging the names of those who were keen enough to call – your name will be on that list.

(Continued)

Careful!

A 'job chat' or 'pre-interview conversation' may be a valuable opportunity for you to find out more about the organisation, but it is also, inevitably, a form of first interview. This is a good thing, but make sure that you follow our guidelines for telephone interviews and make especially sure that you have some pertinent questions to ask. 'Could you tell me something about the job?' is too broad a question and is likely to prompt a fairly banal and superficial answer.

(Continued)

✓ Company brochure (and accounts) – these are public records and can usually be found online. If you are not very familiar with accounts there is perhaps less need to take a look through these, but the company brochure is a useful document because it tells you how the organisation would like to be viewed. Even if you do not mention the brochure explicitly (although this would be impressive), this type of research allows you to interview with a strong sense of the company's sense of identity.

How will I know when my CV is perfect?

Good news – it does not have to perfect! It just has to get you to interview. The easiest way to know whether it works is to use the 'So what?' test. Once you have written and proofread it, leave it to one side for a little while (a few days is ideal), then pick it up again with a 'critical friend' beside you. This might be a friend or family member, or perhaps a work colleague or someone who knows you far less well.

Success checklist

For each section of the CV ask yourself 'So what?' – that is:

✓ Why is this section being included?
✓ Will this section sell you?
✓ Are you wasting space?
✓ Could you replace any of the material in this section with other points that would be more effective in selling you?
✓ Is this the perfect layout for this section or should you add bullet points or additional sub-headings to make it clearer?
✓ Will the person reading it know exactly what you are talking about?
✓ Is that person likely to care about this particular point?

This can seem like a brutal way to review a CV but it will ensure that, when you send it out, it has passed the 'So what?' test and so is the most effective document you can produce.

> **Remember!**
>
> Research completed in America indicates that the average CV review time has gone from 20–30 seconds down to six seconds due to overwhelming numbers of candidates. This means that you need to make your CV stand out whilst being clear to read.

6.3 Covering letters

What is a covering letter?

A 'covering letter' is the letter you send along with a CV or application form to express your interest in a vacancy. Very often, it will actually be a 'covering email' to which you are attaching a CV.

> **Careful!**
>
> Organisations will often advertise several vacancies at the same time, so make sure that you give the reference for the role at the opening of the letter (usually just below the date). If there is no reference, beginning the letter or email by referring to the role will help make sure that it goes to the right place.

When would I need a covering letter?

A covering letter or email gives you the chance to impress upon potential employers just how beneficial it would be to employ you, so do not overlook the chance to produce one. If you are simply asked to email a copy of your CV, there will need to be an email to which to attach it and that is an opportunity for you to impress and persuade. However, there will be cases (such as online application forms) where you might not be given the opportunity to produce a covering letter or CV. In those circumstances, you will want to make the best possible use of the space on an application form that allows you to answer the question 'Why do you think you are suited for this role?' or similar.

How do I begin a covering letter?

If you have carried out research on a particular job, or you have contacted an organisation to ask about opportunities, you will have the ideal starting point – 'Dear Mr Brauner' for example. You will need to use a name if you possibly can, rather than the less impressive 'Dear Sir/Madam'. Even if the advert does not offer the chance of a job chat or similar, it is good practice to ring up and ask for the name of the person to whom a CV or application form should be sent (either by post or email). If you have someone's full name, avoid using it in the clumsy construction 'Dear Ms Emma Braintree' – it is more natural to call her 'Ms Braintree', even if you have spoken to her on the phone.

Top tip

Unless someone particularly signs off on emails or letters as 'Mrs', always formally refer to a woman as 'Ms' unless she has a title such as 'Dr'.

How do I fill up the space on the page?

Be methodical and avoid waffling or blustering. Use an opening sentence, such as 'I am applying for the role of ... '. Take four to six key areas of your skills, experience, personal qualities or achievements and list these after a brief opening ('I feel I am particularly suited to this role because ... ' or 'I feel I could be of value to your organisation as I would bring to the role ... '). Use a bullet-pointed list and, for each of the key areas, give a brief example. That way, each of the bullet points will take up three or four lines. That is all you will need in the central section of the letter, or for the bulk of your email.

Although you will not need to include any more than this, you would use the letter or email to refer to any conversation you have had with the potential employer. So, you might begin with 'Thank you for taking the time to talk to me today. I hope that your train home was not delayed again. After our conversation I am keen to apply for the position ... ' or similar.

Does it matter if I repeat material from my CV?

No – the employer will expect this and it will not be a distraction.

How do I close a covering letter?

As simply as you can and with no pressure on the employer. If you are applying for an advertised position then it is fine to conclude with 'Thank you for taking the time to consider my application form (or CV). I hope to hear from you'. If you are making a speculative approach (that is, not in response to a job advert) it does not work well to end with an expectation placed upon the employer – this can look arrogant. Rather than 'I look forward to hearing from you', it is better to say 'I will contact you next week in the hope that we can discuss this further'. That way, the employer can still call the phone number on the CV, but is not being expected to do anything.

6.4 Application forms

Should I use blue or black ink on an application form?

Probably neither. Most of the time you will not be using ink at all as the vast majority of application forms are now online: these allow you to fill them out, section by section, and save them between sections.

> **Careful!**
>
> It is easy to get carried away with an online application form, enjoying filling out each section neatly and then whizzing on to the next. Take the time to get this right. If the system allows it, you should print out the form first and make a note of what you are going to write in each section. That way you can work through these with confidence.

Having made the point that most applications are online nowadays, this does mean that candidates can be easily flustered if they are asked to complete a paper application form, but it can happen. If you are hoping to work for a smaller organisation, especially if it is for casual or part-time work, a paper application might be expected. If this happens to you, make sure that you do *exactly* what you are asked to do on the form. As with CVs the first aim, when faced with a pile of application forms, is to get rid of those that are unsuitable, and not following basic instructions is one way to make it to the bin fast. Remember that someone has probably spent time and effort in designing the form to give the organisation just the right information, so it will help you too if you can highlight your marketable points in this format.

Are there dangers with an online application form?

If you are filling out an online form there are really only three dangers. You might press 'send' before you finish, you might find the process so quick and easy that you rush through it too fast, and you might struggle if there is no spellcheck in place on the form.

The first two of these dangers is easily avoided if there is the option to download a blank version of the form. That way you can fill it in and gain some practice before you commit to copying and pasting your answers across to the final version. If this option is not available, it can be useful to type out the most important questions in a standard document format and then work on these in advance of filling out the form. This might sound fiddly, and it is, but it is so much better than pressing 'send' and then realising you have made a blunder.

Top tip

The internet browser you use can affect whether spellcheck will work on an online form. Try mistyping a word in the first box you are completing. If spellcheck is clearly not working, try changing your browser.

Given the dangers we have raised around an online form, you might assume that an application form that is a standard Word document – which you download, fill in and upload – would be the safer option. It can be, but make sure that it is not formatted in a way that will jeopardise your application. As you go through keep checking that filling out the boxes is not making any automatic changes to the format of the document overall, and before you send it off print the entire document to reassure yourself that there are no odd page breaks or strange gaps that have emerged as you completed the form.

Can I refer a potential employer to my CV rather than repeating myself?

No. Fill out the form exactly as you are asked.

What if I have nothing to say in one section of the form?

Complete the entire form as best you can and then review the material. It is most likely to be the case that you will be able to shuffle information around so that you can fill all the boxes. So much of the information asked of us in application forms could fit in one or two of the boxes that it is worth spending some time on this. A rewording of information so as to show how appropriate it can be to a box which would otherwise have been left blank is always preferable to an empty box which says nothing positive about you at all.

Could I just send a CV instead?

No. You are working to secure a position and need to follow the route preferred by the organisation.

How do I tackle open questions?

These are the most daunting sections of most application forms and often candidates will whizz through the rest of the form (the 'easy bits') to muster sufficient confidence to complete the large blank section. This can work, but it can also tempt you into rushing through the open questions. These might include 'Why do you think you would be suitable for this role?', 'Why are you applying for this job?', 'What do you hope to gain from this role?' or 'What do you think you can offer our organisation?' The best way to tackle such questions is in advance of even seeing the form. Go to Exercise #24 in the back of the book.

What if there are strange questions on the form?

Application forms do occasionally contain some odd or even slightly aggressive questions. 'How ambitious are you?', for example, or 'Why should we employ you?', or even 'What animal best represents you?' If you are faced with questions such as these, there are two techniques that will help you here:

- Bring the question down to a calmer, more considered version of itself. 'How ambitious are you?' could easily be read as 'Are you interested in further training, or taking advantage of foreign postings we might offer?', whilst 'Why should we employ you?' is actually no different in substance from the gentler question 'What skills, experience and personal qualities would make you a strong candidate?'
- Odd application form questions are often those openings you might usually expect to be offered at interview. If you were asked at interview what animal best represents you, you would automatically look for a genuine answer, but also one which demonstrated the attributes you planned to bring to the role (so, a dog for loyalty and teamwork, for example). Once you see it in that light, odd questions will become easier to answer. Think about what you would say at interview and then use that as the basis for your application answer.

What is the last thing I should do before I send off the form?

The obvious answer to this would be to urge you to proofread the form (and ask someone else to check it for you as well) to make sure that you had not included any errors, but we think that there is one other final check you need to do: check the spacing and structure. It is vital that the first impression an organisation is offered is a positive sense that you have plenty to bring to the role and are certain of exactly how you could benefit that organisation. With that in mind, you need to make sure that you have filled out every single box, if you possibly can, and that you have distributed your material in such a way that there is something of benefit to the employer at every stage of reading the form. Use bullet points or sub-headings if these would be useful in spacing your material more effectively, and do not be afraid to make every line of an open question into a sales point for you – after all, your principal aim is to get an interview.

6.5 Managing the process

It is important to remember that you are in control of the content that you show to potential employers. Your CV is a sales pitch to get you to interview and that interview is an opportunity to show them you are right for the role. To be able to do this effectively, you must research the company (and its connections if it is part of a larger company or in a partnership) so that you can write a targeted CV and covering letter. You should have additional copies of the paperwork that you produce as an aide memoire in interviews or when you are talking to potential employers over the telephone. Always proofread all online forms and written documents that you are producing. Do what is asked of you as that is the first part of the interview process: can you follow instructions? Aim to be honest but show your best side – this is, after all, the professional image that you are trying to capture.

Further reading

As part of managing the process, you might find it useful to do further research using these recommended websites:

6.2 Your CV (Curriculum Vitae)

CV templates:

www.theguardian.com/careers/cv-templates – CV templates for you to use.

www.reed.co.uk/career-advice/blog/2014/january/free-cv-template – More free CV templates that you might want to access.

www.totaljobs.com/careers-advice/cvs-and-applications/which-cv – This offers different CV templates for people who have had a career gap, have had little or lots of work experience, and so on.

www.cv-library.co.uk/cvtemplates – Another CV template, but here you can upload your CV and search for jobs.

https://nationalcareersservice.direct.gov.uk/tools/cv/Pages/default.aspx – National Careers Service CV template.

6.3 Covering letters

Covering letter templates:

www.reed.co.uk/career-advice/blog/2013/november/free-cover-letter-template – This website offers advice about how to compose a covering letter.

www.cv-library.co.uk/coveringletteradvice – This website offers more advice about writing a covering letter.

6.4 Application forms

Advice about different application methods:

https://nationalcareersservice.direct.gov.uk/advice/getajob/applications/Pages/default.aspx – This looks at both online and paper application forms and gives advice about how to fill these in.

www.totaljobs.com/careers-advice/cvs-and-applications/how-to-write-an-application-form – This website gives advice about how to fill in an application form.

Step Seven: Closing the deal

Read this section now if:

- You are getting ready for an interview.
- You have never had a formal interview before and are not sure what to expect.
- You keep getting as far as the interview stage but then do not get the job.
- You are concerned about panel interviews.
- You are being asked to give an interview presentation.
- You have never attended a careers fair.
- You do not find careers fairs useful.
- You are preparing for an assessment day.
- You are worried about being put 'on the spot' by an interviewer.
- The UK is not your home country.

7.1 Introduction: why does it matter?

Whether you are working towards your first or your fourteenth career move, the emphasis is largely the same: you must focus on what you want to do, what you have to offer, and how to find the perfect-looking career move for you. By the time you have done all of that, you can begin to run out of energy and, as a result, a surprising number of candidates for any job are facing the interview stage of the recruitment process with crossed fingers for luck and very little more than that. It is as if they decide simply to fling themselves at the interview in the hope that their brilliant application form or CV will be enough to get them through.

This can work, no doubt, but it is far better to take a deep breath and work this stage of the process as hard as you have worked every other angle.

That means being clear about what is likely to happen to you, being confident that you have prepared for it well enough, and being firm in what *exactly* you are planning to achieve.

Not only will this more robust approach set you up well for the tasks ahead of you, it will also allow you to appreciate that this part of the process is a negotiation. It is not just about you asking someone to give you the chance to prove yourself in their organisation, it is about you looking them in the eye and asking for what you want – and it is even, on occasion, you looking them in the eye and deciding that this is not the right move for you.

In this section we are aiming to do more than simply help you through this stage of recruitment: we want to empower you to make decisions that will work for you in the long term, and then help you develop the skills to make judgements about precisely where you want to be and exactly how to get there.

7.2 Interviews

What types of interviews are there?

You might be interviewed by one person but just as commonly you can end up facing a panel. You might think of interviews as being held in a room, with you and your interviewer(s) facing each other across a table. Rethink! Every single time you are in direct contact with a potential employer, think of this as part of the interview process and apply the same principles to each occasion: thoughtful, prepared, respectful but assertive.

> **Remember!**
>
> If you are given the opportunity to call about whether a job might be right for you before you apply for it, this is still a type of interview, with you assessing the job and the employer beginning to assess you.

How can I make the most of a panel interview?

With the exception of printing off a few more copies of your CV, in case these are needed, your preparation will be exactly the same as for any interview. There are just two golden rules to remember here – at the beginning and end make sure that you make eye contact and/or shake the hand of each panel member, and when you have finished answering a question, regardless of who posed it, look at the whole group to make sure that no-one has a supplementary question.

Top tip

The panel members will not all be expert in your field – there might be a union representative there, or a member of Human Resources, or a colleague from a separate department. Be ready to answer questions from a whole range of people.

How can I prepare for a telephone interview?

If you are able to reimagine this as if it were a face-to-face interview, you will find it easier. If you know in advance when the call will come in, make sure that you are ready five or ten minutes in advance. Have your CV beside you (make sure that it is the version you sent to this employer) along with a glass of water and a notepad with some questions you want to ask (being nervous can mean that even basic questions fly out of your head). Although it will seem a bit odd, dress reasonably smartly; this helps lend a sense of occasion to a telephone interview and will keep your thinking sharp. Similarly, when you are about to answer the call, SMILE! This will come through in your voice and set the right tone for the rest of the call.

Careful!

If an employer calls you up out of the blue and asks to talk to you about your application, this is effectively the first stage interview. Do not be fooled by a casual approach like this – for some people it works well but for many it makes them flustered and they then feel that they are not showing their best side. This type of phone call will usually start with an enquiry as to whether you have time to talk. Even if you feel positive about your application, it is still worth asking the employer to call back in a few minutes, or offer to make the call yourself. This will allow you much needed time to prepare.

What if it is a conference call interview?

You prepare as if for a standard telephone interview, but it can be a good idea to practise with a friend first by setting up a mock conference call interview. Just taking a call on speakerphone with a couple of friends at the other end will give you a sense of how it is going to feel to tackle this challenge.

More than for any other form of interview, make sure that your answers are clearly end-stopped: be brief and clear and then wait for any supplementary question that comes your way. If you cannot hear a question, say so: your confidence will drop if you are not absolutely sure that you are answering the right question. If you cannot hear clearly, ask if it is possible to call them back so that you can try to get a better connection; again, it is better to do this than flounder.

Might I get a video conference interview?

Especially if you are coming to work in the UK, a video conferencing interview (using Skype™ or similar) is a good possibility and you will probably already be thinking in terms of how to succeed in this situation. A video conferencing interview will not be any more onerous than any other type of interview – unless you are not expecting it. If you are in the country in which the job is to be based, you might reasonably expect to be interviewed in person, but if some key members of the interview panel are based abroad, you could find yourself involved in an unexpected video conference interview. If this happens to you, follow all of the guidelines for a panel interview, with one addition: always make sure that, at the end of each answer you give, you glance up at the screen and smile. Candidates at interview often overlook this technique and it is a great way to make the off-site interviewer feel involved and valued.

Remember!

As you are going to prepare for any remote interview situation (telephone interview, video conference call) as if it were face to face, this will include one crucial arrangement: make sure that there is NO CHANCE that you will be interrupted during the event.

How can I prepare for a face-to-face interview?

Success checklist

The four most important questions to ask yourself are:

✓ Have I read through a copy of the right CV, the one I sent to this organisation?
✓ Am I ready to give all of the answers that I can prepare in advance?
✓ Have I mastered a relaxation technique to help me succeed?
✓ What questions would I like to ask at the end of the interview?

What should I do the day before an interview?

> ### Success checklist
>
> The four most important questions you can ask yourself are:
>
> ✓ Do I know where the interview is being held (it might not be at the Head Office or the local branch of the organisation)?
> ✓ Did I confirm, if I was asked to, that I will be attending the interview?
> ✓ Do I have a 'comfort pack' with me (some high energy snacks, a bottle of water, a book so that I can hide in it if I have a long wait, a copy of my CV and/or application form)?
> ✓ Have I got a plan for tonight that lets me relax and get a good night's sleep?

What should I do on the day?

> ### Success checklist
>
> The four most important things to do on the day are:
>
> ✓ Read over your CV and/or application form just once, early in the day, and then resist the temptation to panic yourself by looking at it over again and again – it is not going to change and doing this will just fluster you.
> ✓ If you slept badly, could hardly eat and cannot remember all of the great answers you prepared in advance, ignore this. You are going to have the interview, you will be able to give a good account of yourself, and there will be plenty of time to sleep once you have the job.
> ✓ Leave too much time to get to the venue but make sure that you have something to do once you get there to distract yourself.
> ✓ Turn off your phone just before you go into the interview.

How can I help myself as I wait for my interview?

For some organisations, running just a little behind time on interview days is a deliberate ploy. It gives candidates more time to mentally steel themselves for the challenge ahead (or more time to panic, if they are underprepared) and it also gives the receptionist or other members of staff the chance to sneak a look at the field of hopefuls. The answer to this question, then, is simple. Smile at everyone you see, in a polite rather than a desperate way, and try to avoid talking to other candidates: this can quickly degenerate into a competition. The best way to do this, if you can, is to read whatever company literature is in the reception or interview waiting room, or to read through the internet material about the organisation that you cleverly printed off ready for just this moment.

How can I stop myself panicking as I wait?

Try the relaxation technique in Exercise #25 at the back of the book, which is an extended version of the exercise we offered earlier. We would urge you to practise it at home before the event so that you get into the habit of doing this and know that you can use it well on the day. Although it is effective, it does not need to be intrusive: those around you will hardly notice what you are doing.

What should I do in the first two minutes of an interview?

Whether you are greeted by a single person or a panel, shake hands and smile. This is as much for your benefit as theirs – without even thinking about it, they will smile back at you and that will be the first impression you have of them as you begin to speak. Sit down when you are asked to do so and then make eye contact with the questioner to signal that you are ready to begin. If it is a panel interview, make your first eye contact with the person who introduced you to the other panel members. The first question will probably be intended to put you at your ease, so it might be a simple enquiry about whether you found the building without problems, or if you had a long journey. Even if it appears to be more complicated (someone about why you think you are suitable for the post), try to be succinct in your first answer. The questioner does not want to know about your long and taxing journey, and only wants a brief overview of why you think you are a good fit for the job (always prepare an answer to this sort of standard question in advance).

Remember!

At the end of each question, make eye contact with the questioner to show that you have said what you intended to, but that you are ready to elaborate if needed. If you are in a panel interview, make this eye contact with the person who asked the question but then also glance across at other panel members so that they feel included in the conversation and can take the opportunity to ask you a supplementary question.

What if I get a question that I do not understand?

Interviewers are adept at putting things another way or speaking more clearly if necessary, so do not hesitate to ask for help. Rather than saying that you could not hear (which might embarrass the questioner) or you have no real idea of what is being asked (which might embarrass you) simply ask for the question to be repeated. If you are still unsure, confirm that you have it right ('I think you are asking me to explain how I came to work in retail for a summer?') and wait – usually you will find that the questioner, aware that this could be awkward, will agree to the question you think you are being asked rather than labouring the point, or will rephrase the question entirely so that you can grasp it.

The most usual cause for not understanding a question fully is that it is unexpected – it is easy to get thrown by a question that seems to come out of the blue. Here are some common challenging interview questions that fall into this category. If you have thought through answers to these, you are less likely to be caught out.

Checklist

- *Why do you think I should give you this job?* Obvious, we know, but such a direct question can floor you. Keep your answer succinct and persuasive by focusing on what you can bring to the organisation, not why you think the job might help you in your aims in life.

- *What is your greatest weakness?* It does not help to pretend you have no weaknesses, because we all do, so be honest but offer a positive spin, either by showing how you are working on your areas for development or how, under some circumstances, you have been able to gain something for your employer by what might be thought of as a weakness (see our answer to the question about 'war stories' on page 20).

- *How well do you work under pressure?* You can afford to smile at this one and suggest that they are seeing you under pressure right now. Beyond that, keep it brief – this is not the time to talk about sleepless nights and work problems, but rather to show that you have considered this aspect of work life ('I thrive under pressure, but I do like some fluctuation in the patterns of my work', for example).

- *Why did you leave your last job?* If there is a positive reason that the interviewer(s) will readily understand (I went travelling; I decided to return to study) then this is no problem. If the reason is less positive (I did not get on with my boss; I just could not grasp the requirements of the job; I hated the long hours, for example) then you need to turn this into a convincing 'war story' before you even get to the interview. There is no need to lie, but you can give a better version of the truth ('I wanted a career change

(Continued)

131

(Continued)

and that is why I am so keen to get this job, because … '; 'the job was not quite as it had been advertised and I did not think I could excel there – that is why I am so keen to get this job, because … '; 'I found the hours too rigid for what the job required, which is why I am so pleased to see that you have a more flexible approach to productivity in this workplace').

- *Why have you applied for a job with this organisation?* This seems simple, but it is not simple at all when candidates suddenly realise that they actually know very little about the organisation, or really why they want to work for it. Indeed, they may be applying for so many jobs that they are a bit confused about which organisation does what. Take time to do some research ready for this one and give a very specific answer to prove that you know about the company ('I was really struck by the way you highlighted your local connections in your company brochure, as a local resident myself … '; 'I enjoyed reading the client testimonials on your website – I would like to think that I can provoke that sort of response from your clients in the future').

- *Where do you expect to be in two/five/ten years' time?* Do not be witty and say 'in your seat' – it is a joke that has been worn down over the years and so gives the impression that you are unoriginal and arrogant. Instead, give this some thought in advance and be honest ('I hope I will be in a job that excites me and where I feel I can make a worthwhile contribution'; 'I tend to be a planner so I have thought about this and, in my ideal world, I would have done the training required to succeed in a management role by that time; that is why I am so keen on this job, because I think, with plenty of hard work, I could reach that goal').

- *What salary should we pay you?* Never, ever give a salary figure. You will either be underselling or overvaluing yourself. Instead, be confident but non-specific ('I fulfil the requirements of the job description and person specification, and I have a good level of experience in the field, so I would expect to be at the top end of the scale for this type of work'; 'I recognise that I will need to undertake some training, so I would expect that to be reflected in any offer you make me'). Salary is something to be negotiated once you have the job, never in an interview. If you are pushed to the point where you feel you have no choice but to give a salary figure, hold this as a black mark against the company – do you really want to work for them?

What if I get a question I cannot answer?

Absolutely, positively, DO NOT BLUFF! A little bit of bluffing does no harm, of course. If you are asked if you enjoyed mountain trekking and your single most distinct memory of that trip is curling up, frozen and homesick, in a makeshift tent, it might be reasonable to say 'I enjoyed the camaraderie' (after all, part of the reason for the trip might have been to show an employer that you are a good team player) but if you are asked a direct question that requires knowledge that you just do not have, bluffing can leave you looking both foolish and deceitful. So, if you are asked your view on an organisation's global expansion and it is the first you have heard of it, make this clear in the most positive way possible ('I have not looked into that in detail yet, but I can see how it would make sense, given your UK expansion in recent years' or 'When my previous employer expanded in a similar way it brought some challenges, and I was closely involved in solving some of those on the ground').

Careful!

If you are asked about a qualification you seem to be expected to have, or software with which they seem to think you should be familiar, and you have not heard of these, it is fine to be honest and then point out, with a smile, that you are very keen to train. Offering a whole list of qualifications you do have, as if in compensation, can be off-putting and might suggest that you are criticising the questioner, who you think should have read your CV more carefully.

What if they quiz me on the details on my CV?

You will expect this, so will have prepared for it, but make sure that you are very clear about the CV they have. You will have targeted your CV for different jobs, and if you are going through an agency they might have changed it significantly without your knowledge. Also, take with you a few copies of your CV so that you can distribute these to the interviewer or the interview panel if anything has gone wrong and they do not have a full copy (this happens more often than you might think). If there is one item on your CV that will be a challenge (you need to explain why you do not have a qualification that they said was desirable), be confident by preparing your answer in advance.

What do I do in the last three minutes of an interview?

This is your chance to take control. If you are not asked if you have any questions, do not ask any. If you are asked if you have any questions, do not see this as an opportunity to quiz them on the details of the job, and consider whether this is really the time and place to ask about the salary details, the holiday entitlement or their private health cover (we would say not). Instead, think of brief but interesting questions that show how committed you are to your development and their organisation, and make sure they are questions that call for brief answers. These might include the following.

Success checklist

✓ 'You mentioned that you are expanding your operation here in Manchester – it sounds exciting. What is the timeframe for that?'

✓ 'I was interested when you talked about training for the job. Can you tell me a little more about that?'

✓ 'I noticed from your website that you operate a 'Fun Friday' policy – it sounds intriguing! What is it?'

✓ 'When we were talking about the person specification just now you said that some First Aid experience would be really useful in the role. I was a designated First Aider in my last job – was this the type of thing you were thinking of?'

✓ 'I know that one of your key requirements is being able to deal with members of the public; I have experience in that area, as we have already discussed, but I am not clear about exactly how this works in your organisation – would this be at public events or when members of the public are visiting the office?'

✓ 'As we have just been discussing, I really enjoy working direct with clients. I can see that that is going to be useful in this role. Will much of it be face to face, or do you tend to work mainly by email? I have experience of both, but just want to get a clearer idea of that part of the role.'

Top tip

If you genuinely do not have any questions, that is fine. Avoid bluffing and making up a random question on the spot. Instead, smile and say that you think they have answered any question you might have had, thank you.

Once you have asked your questions and they have offered their answers, thank them and smile. Shake hands with everyone in the room (even if they are not all looking like they expect this) and leave calmly. DO NOT speed up as you get near the door – this is too big a clue as to how relieved you are feeling that the ordeal is behind you. A steady walk indicates that it was a challenge, but that you were happy to meet it.

How should I leave the building?

You would be amazed at how many people actually jog away from the building, or burst into tears (of relief or horror), or loiter in the entrance for five minutes texting their friends, or call a friend and talk loudly about the interview in the lift down to the entrance. Do none of these things. Smile at anyone you see as you are walking out of the interview area and maintain a steady pace until you are sure that you are out of sight of everyone in the building. Then you can allow yourself a little hop of happiness that it is over and you have done a good job.

What if I do not get the job?

Call the organisation and ask why you were not successful. It would be reassuring to learn that, in the end, no-one was appointed because of a major restructuring, or that someone with ten years' more experience than you got the job. Knowing this means you will not fall into the trap of blaming yourself. Equally, it is useful to be told that your interview technique needs work – the more specific feedback you can get, the better.

7.3 Interview presentations

Who might see my presentation?

This varies hugely. Sometimes just one person will see a presentation, but it might be seen by many more people than will interview you, so that a whole department can evaluate candidates' presentations.

Top tip

If you are not told how many people will see your presentation, you could ask for numbers so that you can prepare enough handouts in advance.

What topics might I cover?

This might not be as you expect – quite commonly candidates are asked to present on any topic they like, or are specifically asked not to present on the job for which they are applying or a past professional situation. Make sure that you fully understand the remit (and it is acceptable to call and ask for clarification if you are unsure) and then plan to show your best side through your presentation. Although you will be judged on how well you present and how professional your handouts look, there will also, inevitably, be an assessment of how you would fit into a team. A presentation on your solo trip to Australia for six months might show that you are determined, adventurous and resourceful, but it will not instantly shout 'team player' unless you also add that you worked your way around the country, usually as part of tight-knit fruit-picking teams.

Careful!

Avoid the trap of assuming that being given an open brief really means that you can talk about anything, however outlandish (perhaps just to them) or humorous (perhaps just to you). Think about which personal qualities and skills you want to display, about the level of interest the audience might have in your presentation topic, and crucially, ask around to see how your family and friends respond to your idea for a presentation.

Should I use presentation aids?

This will be one of the first questions you will ask when you are given the brief. It would be relatively unusual (but not unheard of nowadays) for you to give a presentation with no aids whatsoever. Presentation aids that might help you give a successful presentation include the following.

Success checklist

✓ A data projector with associated software (such as PowerPoint™ or Prezi™): PowerPoint™ is standard, but Prezi™ can give a more creative feel to what you are doing. Take control of the software and be confident – insipid PowerPoint™ presentations are boring and badly designed Prezi™ presentations can have vertiginous effect.

✓ The internet: a hugely powerful tool, of course, but perhaps risky unless you can be certain that there is full internet access at the moment you are presenting and that the page you want to display will not have disappeared overnight. If the page has no moving images, use a screenshot to make a spare handout, just in case.

✓ Interactive whiteboard: only use this to its full potential if you have experience – they can be tricky.

✓ Handouts: useful for ensuring that the audience has some good 'take-away information' from your presentation but avoid making handouts so detailed that they are daunting. Never offer a boring handout – produce it to a professional standard and remember that this is the lasting impression of your presentation your viewers will get.

✓ Demonstrations: these can be hugely effective, if practised sufficiently in advance. Make sure that you film the demonstration so that if it fails on the day you can show the film instead.

✓ You: you are always your principal presentation aid, so focus on giving the best possible impression regardless of the presentation aids you might be using. That way, nothing can distract you too much on the day.

Remember!

However well you prepare, technology can let you down at the last minute, so always have a back-up plan ready. No-one will mind looking at a handout rather than the screen, as long as you explain the problem, move on and smile. They will feel guilty that their technology failed, and admiring of your determination to succeed regardless.

How long might an interview presentation last?

It will usually be between 10 and 30 minutes for most jobs that you are likely to be considering. Always make sure that you are given a clear time limit to which you can work and practise to a couple of minutes under that limit.

Careful!

You will be judged not just on your how you present, but also on how well you use your resources and your time. It will not matter if you finish a minute or so under the allotted time, but it will be a disaster if you go over. This is one of the biggest pitfalls in presenting – avoid it!

How do I prepare?

Practise, practise, practise! However you usually prepare for a presentation (and if you have not given a presentation before, now is a good time to ask for help from someone more experienced than you), rehearsal is going to be key. The rehearsal schedule in Exercise #26 works well and we recommend you take a look at this.

What about my nerves?

The technique we offered in our earlier answer on tackling nerves when you are about to be interviewed will work equally well for interview presentations.

Would a presentation be part of the actual interview?

Not necessarily. There might be a series of presentations given by candidates in the morning, with a series of interviews in the afternoon. You should be given a schedule for the day and this will give you the information you need. If you are unsure, ask for clarification.

What is the worst thing that could happen?

You forget to smile. That might sound like a glib answer, but experience suggests that audience members watching interview presentations will not worry too much about anything going wrong, as long as the presenter does not make them feel bad about it. Smiling at the audience members proves you are in control, and will show that you are keen despite any glitches. Remember that this is a group of human beings and they want to recruit a good team member. If you scowl at them or look as if you do not like them, they cannot help but look elsewhere for their new colleague. 'The candidate felt like one of us' is one of the most common and compelling reasons given for employing anyone.

7.4 Recruitment/careers fairs

What is a recruitment or careers fair?

An event run by your university/college where employers come to talk to students about the opportunities available in their organisations. They might be given either name but these are the same. There are usually plenty of stands and displays to wander around to offer you inspiration, as well as opportunities to find out about specific career openings.

Someone mentioned the 'milk round' – what is that?

The milk round used to be the system by which large organisations would visit universities and colleges annually to recruit students. This has now been replaced by careers fairs.

What sort of companies might be there?

Companies that want to recruit. That is all you need worry about – the rest you will find out at the event or in your preparation. As this day really could change your life, you will want to invest some time in finding out what is being offered and how you might fit into an organisation. To find out what you need to be doing when you attend one of these events, go to Exercise #27 at the back of the book.

> **Careful!**
>
> Not everyone representing a company at a recruitment fair will be expert in every aspect of the organisation. We have had experience in the past of people finding the company reps a bit daunting or even off-putting because they had no idea, for example, that a technical author needs to be a good communicator, rather than a scientist. Do your homework in advance and be brave.

Are recruitment fairs only for students?

They can be, and that can be their huge advantage from a student's point of view. However, there are also more general recruitment and careers fairs that are open to all, so keep a look out for these.

What if there are no companies there that want my skills?

There will be – look below the surface. At least 85% of organisations at careers fairs want any and all types of qualification areas. This makes sense, once you think about it. Science firms need in-house lawyers, technical authors and HR specialists; design companies need accountants; publishers need logistic experts. The biggest loss in careers fairs is the loss of potential employees to any industry because they just did not know that they had to look past the obvious to find the real jobs. Never allow yourself to be one of those people.

What if no companies there match my career plans?

Be flexible – you will have to be once you hit the career market, and this is a great place to start because there is so much on offer. If you want to be a journalist, for example, and cannot see a news outlet there, then this is your chance to ask about writing opportunities in organisations (in-house journalism is now huge, and marketing firms need good writers).

What should I look out for?

You might find that a Careers Service is offering drop-in sessions during the day – these can be a good way to soak up plenty of useful advice in one event. When you are looking around the stands, look for someone you can talk to rather than just picking up a leaflet. This could become a mini-interview which might get you ahead of other people who apply more formally later.

Should I take anything with me?

The more you can demonstrate how much this matters to you the more likely you are to stick in the mind of the company reps, and the more written material you give them the more probable it is that they will put your details on file for recruitment. Avoid offering them a wodge of irrelevant material, but offer a CV at the least.

What should I wear?

This can be tricky. Wearing your best professional outfit might make you (and the company reps) feel uncomfortable, but too casual and they will assume that you just wandered in on your way to meeting some friends and have no real interest. Go for smart but not a suit – unless your Careers Service has recommended otherwise.

How should I act?

With purpose. A brief walk around, but then straight to business, approaching each of your target organisations one by one, ready to ask a question (from your prepared list) and also to answer their questions.

> **Remember!**
>
> Any conversation with an organisation's representatives is a form of selection – you are seeing if you like them and they are judging whether you would fit in with their team, so be bold in selling yourself in this arena. Assume it is a form of first interview if they have a conversation with you, but do not be downhearted if they simply want to offer you information and take your details. These events can get busy so sometimes that is all they can do on the day.

7.5 Assessment days

What is an assessment day?

Sometimes called a selection or interview day, this involves more than just an interview. You might also be asked to give a presentation, or work with others to give a group presentation; you could be offered a tour of an organisation, or asked to join potential colleagues for a meal. It would not be unusual to be expected to join in with some group activity for part of the day; this might be linked to the work you would be doing or perhaps a more generic team-building exercise.

How can I prepare?

Success at days such as this relies heavily on being prepared, so reassure yourself by finding out as much as you can before the day.

Success checklist

✓ Where is the event being held and how long will it last?
✓ Will everyone be expected to be there all day, or is the afternoon being spent in running second interviews just for some?
✓ Will my expenses be paid? (This might sound a bit blunt, but it could be an expensive risk if you are paying for everything yourself and it is several hundred miles away.)
✓ If it is a whole day event, will there be somewhere to get lunch?
✓ Should I prepare anything ahead of time (such as a presentation)?
✓ Would it be useful to bring additional material? (This might be a research project or portfolio of your work.)

Remember!

Always take a few spare copies of your CV with you regardless of what they suggest you might need – they can get lost in the system or be photocopied for the interviewers with a page missing.

How do I react to group exercises or games?

This will depend on the role for which you are applying and the person you want them to see, but the key is balance. Even if you are being considered for a high pressure sales job, they could still want to see that you can be a member of the team rather than simply a killer salesperson; if you are being tested for leadership skills, they will recognise that listening is more effective than shouting for any leader. You will have researched the organisation thoroughly and pondered over both the job description and person specification. You are convinced that you are right for the job, which makes the answer simple: be yourself, aware of those around you and the needs of the day, and avoid exhausting yourself by pretending to be other than you are. They have selected you to attend this day, so you must be the type of person they need.

If they provide a lunch or dinner, should I go to it?

Yes, but do not allow yourself to be lulled into thinking that it is just a nice social occasion. Every activity on the day is designed to assess how well candidates would fit the role, and that includes how well you would fit into the team as a person, beyond any skills or experience you are offering. This is actually a good thing, because it gives you the chance to do some assessing of your own. If you sit down to a meal with a group of your future colleagues and you do not like the way they talk about work, or the bosses, or life in general, you should begin to wonder whether this is the job for you. They will not be your only colleagues, of course, but an unpleasant social time would make you wonder.

How can I stand out, even if I am nervous?

Funnily enough, a few moments of thoughtful silence can be your best asset. Rather than rushing to answer every question or leaping into action the moment your group is asked to do something, take a moment's pause to consider your next answer or your next move. That way, you can make sure that you give your very best answer, or you volunteer only to do something that you know will be successful.

Top tip

This works well in interviews, too. Interviewers are often most impressed by the candidate who will occasionally pause after a question to consider the best way to answer it fully.

What if they ask me to do something unexpected on the day?

This happens. You might find a request on the day rather unusual, but this is not something to worry about. A change in the timing of activities or being asked to write a short review of an event that has taken place – these things will be a challenge, but you are ready for that. If the request seems off or makes you feel uncomfortable, think before you agree. It would not be unreasonable to ask you to show your telephone technique for a brief mock phone call, but asking you to spend an entire afternoon making sales calls or answering customer complaints would be questionable. Asking you to get involved in a team activity would be fine, but expecting you to bully other candidates during the process so that you can emerge triumphant would make you far less happy with yourself and the organisation. Whatever the pressure to make a success of the day, try to remember that a selection process is two-way. You only want to work for an organisation you trust and with people you respect.

7.6 Managing the process

Smile. A smile is the best way for you to relax because you will find that people smile back. It also makes you look confident and in control even if you are not! Take your time when preparing for an interview, answering questions or formulating your own questions to ensure that you get this right. Use relaxation techniques as a routine before doing anything that you find scary: these will help you mentally prepare for the challenge and give you something to occupy yourself with rather than focusing on the next thing. Being prepared is one of the greatest secrets to success.

> **Remember!**
>
> Selection is a two-way process. You may come away from an encounter feeling that the job is not for you and it is better to admit that straightaway rather than going down the wrong career path.

Further reading

As part of managing the process, you may find it useful to do further research using the recommended websites listed below.

7.2 Interviews

How to handle different types of interviews:

http://career-advice.monster.com/job-interview/interview-preparation/prepare-for-different-interview-types/article.aspx – This website gives advice about tackling different types of interviews.

https://careers.usc.edu/docs/handouts/Interview_Different_Types.pdf – This is a PDF file that explains different types of interviews so that you can feel prepared before you go into an interview.

7.3 Interview presentations

How to prepare and deliver a successful interview presentation:

www.jobs.ac.uk/careers-advice/interview-tips/2131/10–top-tips-for-interview-presentations –
This offers tips on how to put together an excellent interview presentation.
www.totaljobs.com/careers-advice/interviews/tips-for-interview-presentations – This website
offers more advice about how to prepare your interview presentation.

7.4 Recruitment/careers fairs

Finding a job fair:

www.thejobfairs.co.uk – This website gives you information about various job fairs that
you might want to attend in the UK.
http://jobfairsin.com – This website gives you information about various job fairs that you
might want to attend in the USA.
www.globalcareersfair.com – This website looks at job opportunities across the globe and
allows you access to them.

7.5 Assessment days

Find out more about what assessment days involve and how to make the most of them:

www.assessmentday.co.uk/assessmentcentre/index.html – This explains what assessment
centres are and prepares you for experiencing an assessment for a job.
www.jobs.ac.uk/careers-advice/interview-tips/1821/surviving-the-assessment-centre – This
offers you more information about what to expect if you are invited to an assessment
centre as part of the application process.

Conclusion: Learning to enjoy it

This has been quite a journey. We have walked with you through self-analysis, networking, researching the career market and making your first steps into it. We have offered advice on how to sell your skills, experience and qualities into that career market, negotiating and judging as you go so that you make the best move for you with the brightest possible future. Once you have reached that stage there is one last secret that we would like to share with you. Take a moment. Take several moments. Look around you – what do you see? If there are things you would like to change, now that you have achieved this goal, there is no reason why you cannot make plans to do this. If your current location is just one step on the career path you plan to take, remind yourself of where you are heading so that you do not lose sight of the goal. If you made a compromise in this career move you will already be considering how to mitigate the effects of that compromise, moving yourself to a better position in the coming weeks and months. These are not problems, and they are certainly not career mistakes, they are just part of a process. If, when you look about, everything is as you want it to be, even if just for now, enjoy it!

Exercises

EXERCISE #1: How can I tell how near my work self is to my true self?

Answer the following questions where you can, and if you are unsure of the answer, ask friends or colleagues to help:

1. Do you generally enjoy your workplace (not the work itself, necessarily, but the fact of going to work or study in that place)?
2. When you are in a group situation, do you usually feel that your voice is being heard?
3. Do you think that those around you have their voices heard when you are all together?
4. Do you often forget the time as you work?
5. Do you occasionally work through part of your break time, or stay on later than you had planned, just to get some study or work project completed?
6. Do you sleep well on a Sunday night?
7. Do you feel that the requirements of your current situation give you the chance to show off your abilities?
8. Are you sometimes the first person asked to carry out a task?
9. Do your friends think that you are studying or doing the job that they expected of you?
10. Did your family support you when you tried to get into your current position of work or study, rather than having any reservations?
11. Do you recognise yourself as being content with the way in which you are working or studying?
12. Do you tend to enjoy all the various parts of your day?
13. Are you happy to have friends and family meet you in your place of work or study – are you comfortable interacting with them in that setting?

Careful!

The indicators highlighted by this exercise can be caused by overwork or an unpleasant boss or tutor, which is why we would urge you to answer 'no' only if you are aware of a persistent problem.

Now that you have completed the exercise, what should you do about it? If you answered 'no' to several of these questions, be ready to use the techniques we will be offering in this book to reimagine the career you could have. If you answered 'yes' to all (or nearly all) of the questions, you can safely rely more on your own experience and replicate most aspects of your current position when you come to look for your next role.

EXERCISE #2: How can I get a better picture of my career self?

1. Look through your job description, if you are already in work – this will tell you what you should be doing.
2. Check your appraisal either in work or in study – this will tell you what you *have* been doing. Going back to the job description, highlight all of the qualities outlined in this that you feel you match most of the time in your favourite colour.
3. Next, highlight all of the qualities outlined that you feel you match some of the time in your next favourite colour.
4. Highlight all of the qualities you rarely (or do not) match in the colour you like least. You should now have a better understanding of which qualities you have and which qualities you may need to develop.
5. Consider the additional tasks you are asked to perform in your work or study – for example, do you tend to organise social gatherings, or find additional resources for projects?
6. How do you react to meetings, seminars or study groups? Do you usually end up being the chairperson, or do you prefer to contribute?
7. Do people come to you for new ideas, or to help complete projects, or to deal with the detail?
8. Rather than just asking those who manage you to share with you a sense of how you are perceived by others, try also asking a close colleague with whom you have worked.
9. Ask someone who is not involved in your day-to-day activity but knows you by reputation (perhaps someone in a different department or on a different course from you).
10. Create a new job description and/or person specification for the job/course of study you are doing now – does it sound like you?
11. Look at job adverts for vacancies that are broadly similar to your own job or the jobs you are currently pursuing – which aspects of the roles being described appeal to you most?
12. Write down seven key qualities that you have, for which you now have proof. These will not only help you search for the most appropriate career they will also help you when it comes to applications and interviews, as you will now be able to show evidence of those qualities.
13. Pat yourself on the back and relax safe in the knowledge that you have just begun to identify your personal qualities and that you will never accidently apply for a job that will make you feel miserable.

EXERCISE #3: Creating an experience inventory

1. Produce a table that has four columns and a variable amount of rows (you will not know yet exactly how many rows you will need).
2. In the first column, write out a list of all of the sections of your life from the age of 14 (so this might be a period of time at school, then perhaps college and/or university, then maybe some voluntary or paid work, followed perhaps by time away from work for various reasons, then it might be that you have returned to the workplace).
3. Against each of these, in the second column, write down what you did that was not a qualification but was still useful experience. For example, you would not list the courses you did at school to gain qualifications, but you would list being a member of a debating society or charity group. If you have had time away from the workplace you would list any activity that you feel could be of benefit to an employer because it has developed you as a person or increased your skills base. If you were in a job, your job title would not be relevant here, but the experiences of your day-to-day work life would provide material for this column.

This can seem like an endless task and, even though you are talking about your own life and you know that it is important to gather this material together, it is easy to get bored and skip on the detail, or to feel that you are being overly boastful about yourself. Take plenty of breaks and, ideally, keep returning to this exercise over a few days so you can be sure that you have captured enough material. You will only have to do this once, so it is worth the effort. When this is complete, keep it somewhere safe so that you can add to it from time to time rather than starting from the beginning when you next need it.

4. Go back and look at each experience you have listed and, where you can, make a note in column three of the ways in which this experience brought a benefit to someone else. This need not be an employer, although in many cases it is likely to be. You do not have to be able to do this for every piece of experience you have had, but it will help show the value of your experience to an organisation if you are able to point to how you have brought some benefit to situations in the past.

The benefits you include in your table might not all be about others – you can also usefully include benefits that you have accrued for yourself. So, for example, the person organising the pub quiz below might find an increased confidence in talking in public as a result of running the event, and this is listed in the table alongside the benefit to the employer.

5. Finally, against a selection of your experiences, jot down a few words that would remind you of a 'war story' you could offer at interview: that is, an example of your experience in action and the way it was of benefit.

Here is an example of an experience inventory in the process of being completed, highlighting only the time that the person was in college:

Life section	Experience	Benefit	War story
School			
College	Charity action group fundraiser	Raised charity income by 16%	Setting up an exhibition at the local County Show
College	Carer for elderly relative		Working with the local authority to ensure the smooth delivery of services
College	Study group leader		
College	Part-time work in a bar serving customers	Increased number of customers on a Wednesday night Improved self-confidence	Setting up and running a pub quiz each Wednesday
University			
Travelling, teaching abroad			
Job 1			
Job 2			
Career break			

You will notice that not every column is filled in for each section, and that is fine. It may be that the person filling out the form feels that there is enough material here already, or perhaps a return to working on the table is planned for the coming weeks and months, as examples and recollections come to mind.

6. Now make the chart work for you. Each time you are facing the challenge of applying for a vacancy, or approaching an organisation direct for a discussion about possible openings, go back to a fresh copy of your chart and highlight those sections of experience that seem most valuable to you in selling yourself into your target organisation or role. There will hopefully be quite a bit of highlighting across the table, but restrict yourself to just a few of the war stories (see page 20) being highlighted: you will not have the opportunity to use every 'war story' at your disposal.

EXERCISE #4: What do employers want?

1. Imagine you ran the type of organisation you would like to employ you. You may find it helpful to research organisations that you are interested in so that you are better informed to do the following tasks. Write a brief summary about the organisation, including its mission statement.
2. Consider what you would be looking for to fulfil the role for which you are applying.

3. Now write a list of all of the facets (qualities, skills, qualifications and experience) you would ask for in an employee. If you are getting a bit stuck, look at the job adverts produced by the organisation and this will help you understand what they require.
4. Prioritise them by writing numbers next to each of these starting from 1 (the most important). Remember that you are still thinking from the point-of-view of the organisation.
5. Analyse why you think these things are important. Where is the evidence? From job adverts? From working in that industry? From talking with people already working in that field? By analysing why you have decided that 'communication skills' is the top quality looked for by the organisation, you will prevent yourself from being too subjective. It might be that you think communication skills are important because you are most proud of your own communication skills, in which case you may need to re-evaluate the order you have created.
6. Have your priorities changed?
7. Next to each of the listed qualities, write down some ideas of when you have demonstrated them. Although it is tempting to focus just on your work history, you should also look at a wider range of experiences that may afford you some evidence of you demonstrating these qualities.

Well done! Now you are much better prepared to answer questions about your qualities, with supporting examples of them in practice.

EXERCISE #5: What might motivate me?

1. Write a list of intrinsic motivators, for example: 'I enjoy being organised'.
2. Write a list of extrinsic motivators, for example: 'I want to command a good salary'.
3. Decorate your lists with pictures that will motivate you such as photos of family, drawings of money, smiley faces, and so forth; whenever you glance at one of these, you will smile.
4. Keep all these lists nearby so that you will see them every day to remind you why you are not giving up.

It can be difficult to generate your own ideas about what might motivate you, so we have listed some common sources of motivation (both intrinsic and extrinsic) to get you started. Remember that each motivator could also be a demotivator. The chance to travel, for example, could fill you with dread, especially if you interpret it as driving up the motorway each day in a lengthy commute! Once you get going you are likely to come up with more:

- The chance to travel.
- Flexible working hours.
- The possibility of working from home at times.
- A teamworking situation.
- A good salary or the chance of rapid promotion to a good salary.
- The opportunity to train.
- Working with like-minded people.
- Meeting a range of new people.
- Dealing with members of the public.

- A sense of service to your local area or the global community.
- An intellectual challenge.
- Prestige and a career that will impress.
- Doing something your parents did before you.
- Using your qualities (creativity, for example, or your sense of good order).
- Putting your skills, training and education to good use.
- Having an easy life, or having a challenging life.
- Working in a large organisation.
- Working outdoors or indoors.
- Variety in your working day.
- A sense of excitement with new challenges appearing regularly.
- Some unpredictability in what you will be expected to do.
- Job security.
- A clear career structure.
- Independence and autonomy.
- A career that suits your family's needs.

EXERCISE #6: How do I pull the skills out of a situation?

1. Choose a situation and write a sentence or two about what happened.
2. Think about the skills you demonstrated during that situation. You may find the list of examples below helpful as you get started.

What happened?	The skill that was demonstrated
I took notes during the meeting and then typed them up afterwards.	Literacy, an ability to take concise and accurate notes, organisational skills.
I contributed during the meeting by updating the team on what I had been doing.	Public speaking skills and verbal reporting.
I arrived at the meeting early to check that the room was set up so that we could start on time.	Time-keeping skills.
When a problem arose with my colleague's computer so that he could not give his presentation, I helped him fix it.	Technology skills.
We discussed a problem with a project we were working on and I helped to come up with a workable solution.	Problem-solving skills.

EXERCISE #7: Creating a skills inventory

Unlike an experience inventory, we are not suggesting here that you list every single time you have used or developed a skill, but you will still need to produce a table, this time with four columns.

1. In Column 1, list a situation in which you would have had to use a skill (this will not be an entire job or area of your life, but a more closely defined situation, such as working with a study group or chairing a meeting).

Top tip

Even at this stage you might find this difficult to maintain – it can be unexpectedly draining to analyse your life in this way. Take plenty of breaks between bouts of activity on this – it does not necessarily matter if it takes you several days to work up your skills inventory.

2. In Column 2, list the skills involved in every situation, giving each skill a separate line. For example, chairing a meeting might have involved using cloud-based software to arrange the meeting time (Skill 1 – IT), the collation of appropriate documents (Skill 2 – administration), giving an opening presentation about the meeting topic (Skill 3 – presentation skills), making sure that everyone had the chance to speak and that nobody got too carried away (Skill 4 – negotiation), and keeping the meeting to time (Skill 4 – time management). The exercise above on pulling the skills out of a situation will help you with this. Make sure that, for each time you list a skill, you list the situation in Column 1 again, so that you can reorder your table later if you want to without losing the thread between situation and skill.

Top tip

Do not worry if, at this early stage, you feel that you are not picking up the strongest example of using a skill – that will come later.

3. In Column 3, list beside your skills any benefits that you were able to bring to a situation as a result of your skills.

Top tip

You will not be able to do this against every skill, and that is fine – you just need a few examples for your 'war stories' (see page 20) at interview.

4. Once you have listed a good number of your situations and identified the skills you developed or used within those situations, you are ready to bring it all together. In Column 4, number the first skill you listed and then note down the number (so, in the example we used for Column 2 above, 'IT skills' is now numbered as Skill 1). Work through each skill listed and put a new number beside it if you have not mentioned it

before, or put the appropriate number beside it if you have already numbered it earlier. So, for example, you might by the end have a dozen skills with '1' noted beside them because, even though the situations were different, you demonstrated IT skills in each circumstance.

Top tip

It would be nigh on impossible to list every single situation in your study, home, social and work lives in which you have demonstrated a skill, nor do you need to do this. You will find that, as your inventory progresses, you will naturally begin to list only those skills that really stand out in a situation. This is a good thing as it means you are prioritising those situations that will offer you the strongest example of your skills development or your skills in action.

6. People respond in different ways to their skills inventories. Some prefer to leave it like this, finding it easier that way to trace their skills back through situations. Others prefer to start moving things around in the table, so that all the examples of each skill are bunched together.

Top tip

Assuming that you are producing this on a computer, keep a separate, original copy before you start to reorder so that if you do not find it easy to work with the reordered table you can revert back to drawing information from your original.

Here is an example of a skills inventory in its early stages, showing just three example situations:

Situation	Skills	Benefits (your war stories for interview)	Skill ordering
Chairing weekly meetings – arrange them	Cloud-based IT	Greater attendance at the meetings because everyone could negotiate the timing	1
Chairing weekly meetings – collating the paperwork	Filing and collating		2

Situation	Skills	Benefits (your war stories for interview)	Skill ordering
Chairing weekly meetings – opening presentation	Presenting	Persuaded members of the group to adopt a new approach to a situation by a persuasive presentation	3
Chairing weekly meetings – letting everyone have their say	Negotiating		4
Chairing weekly meetings – keeping to time	Time management		5
Producing a report on time in the correct format	Report writing		6
Producing a professional-looking report	IT		1
Producing a report on time	Time management		5
Producing a report on time with enough evidence to persuade	Analysis	I got a good mark/a promotion at work as a result of the report	7
Producing a report on time with a strong argument	Articulating arguments	People took action as a result of the report	8
Arranging a charity event – getting people involved	Team building	Raised £10,000 for charity	9
Arranging a charity event – getting people involved	Leadership		10
Arranging a charity event – producing all of the publicity material	IT		1
Arranging a charity event – keeping accurate records for the charity	Record keeping		2
Arranging a charity event – arranging the venue at a discounted price	Negotiating		4
Arranging a charity event – giving a vote of thanks speech	Presenting	I was asked to arrange a similar event the following year	3

Now here is an example of the same three situations, and the skills attached to them, reordered by skills rather than by situation:

Situation	Skills	Benefits (your war stories for interview)	Skill ordering
Chairing weekly meetings – arrange them	Cloud-based IT	Greater attendance at the meetings because everyone could negotiate the timing	1
Producing a professional-looking report	Microsoft IT		1
Arranging a charity event – producing all of the publicity material	Web-based IT		1
Chairing weekly meetings – collating the paperwork	Filing and administration		2
Arranging a charity event – keeping accurate records for the charity	Record keeping		2
Chairing weekly meetings – opening presentation	Presenting	Persuaded members of the group to adopt a new approach to a situation by a persuasive presentation	3
Arranging a charity event – giving a vote of thanks speech	Presenting	I was asked to arrange a similar event the following year	3
Chairing weekly meetings – letting everyone have their say	Negotiating		4
Arranging a charity event – arranging the venue at a discounted price	Negotiating		4
Chairing weekly meetings – keeping to time	Time management		5
Producing a report on time	Time management		5
Producing a report on time in the correct format	Report writing		6
Producing a report on time with enough evidence to persuade	Analysis	I got a good mark/a promotion at work as a result of the report	7
Producing a report on time with a strong argument	Articulating arguments	People took action as a result of the report	8
Arranging a charity event – getting people involved	Team building	Raised £10,000 for charity	9
Arranging a charity event – getting people involved	Leadership		10

Top tip

You will probably have noticed that not every skill exactly matches the others in its group – so IT is Skill 1, but there are various forms of IT listed. This is a good thing, as it allows you to begin to see your skills base as comprising groups of interrelated skills. This will make you a more convincing candidate in the selection process and allow you more flexibility in interview discussions.

7. When you have reached this stage, you can begin to be selective about your 'war stories' (see page 20). It makes sense to have a few to tell, but you might decide, for example, that in the case of 'presenting' in the skills inventory above, the example of a benefit arising from chairing the weekly meeting is stronger than the example taken from the charity event. By highlighting that example, you will have a list of war stories to hand ready for later stages in the process:

Situation	Skills	Benefits (your war stories for interview)	Skill ordering
Chairing weekly meetings – arrange them	Cloud-based IT	Greater attendance at the meetings because everyone could negotiate the timing	1
Producing a professional-looking report	Microsoft IT		1
Arranging a charity event – producing all of the publicity material	Web-based IT		1
Chairing weekly meetings – collating the paperwork	Filing and administration		2
Arranging a charity event – keeping accurate records for the charity	Record keeping		2
Chairing weekly meetings – opening presentation	Presenting	**Persuaded members of the group to adopt a new approach to a situation by a persuasive presentation**	3
Arranging a charity event – giving a vote of thanks speech	Presenting	I was asked to arrange a similar event the following year	3

(Continued)

(Continued)

Situation	Skills	Benefits (your war stories for interview)	Skill ordering
Chairing weekly meetings – letting everyone have their say	Negotiating		4
Arranging a charity event – arranging the venue at a discounted price	Negotiating		4
Chairing weekly meeting – keeping to time	Time management		5
Producing a report on time	Time management		5
Producing a report on time in the correct format	Report writing		6
Producing a report on time with enough evidence to persuade	Analysis	I got a good mark/a promotion at work as a result of the report	7
Producing a report on time with a strong argument	Articulating arguments	**People took action as a result of the report**	8
Arranging a charity event – getting people involved	Team building	**Raised £10,000 for charity**	9
Arranging a charity event – getting people involved	Leadership		10

By the time you have completed the first few situations in your skills inventory you will be feeling more confident, more secure in your skills base, and ready to talk about skills convincingly at interview.

EXERCISE #8: Which skills should I focus on boosting?

1. Take the job description and person specification of a target job. This does not have to be a real job you are going for – it might be similar to one that you have heard about that appeals to you. You may prefer to take a selection of documents relating to a career area that you would like to target (job descriptions, adverts, person specifications, online job outlines and so forth) and work from an amalgamation of them. List the most important skills that are required, and put them on a spiderweb chart so that it looks similar to this:

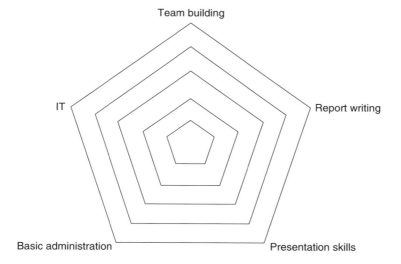

2. Even though you have chosen the essential skills for a role or career area, these are not all going to be equally important, so now use the spiderweb chart to show their relative importance. For example, like this:

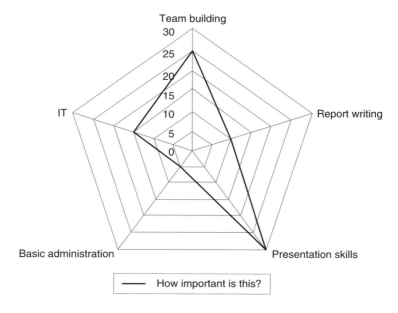

3. Now superimpose the level of skill you have in each area, like this:

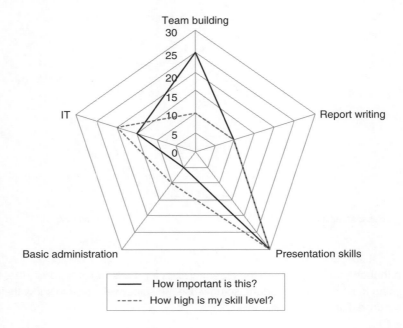

4. It will now be a simple matter to assess where you have the necessary level of skill, where you have more than is required, and where you are a little below the levels that the position might demand.

In this example, the candidate will be happy that there is a good match on presentation skills, which are a major requirement of the role, and report writing, which is of less importance in this role but is still pleasing to have. The candidate exceeds expectations in the IT and administrative sides of the role, but needs to develop team-building skills, which are an important part of the role.

5. For those areas where you meet or exceed expectations, you will be able to refer back to your skills and experience inventories to begin to identify the best 'war stories' for this job or career area.

EXERCISE #9: What training should I invest in?

If you are going to invest time and money in studying or training, it makes sense to get the best deal, not just now but also in terms of the long-term advantages you can expect for your effort. Take these steps to ensure that you get ahead:

1. Use your networks to find out what professionals in your target career area would recommend in terms of training. Remember that Alumni Associations or social media sites linked to schools or colleges can be useful in this regard – talking to those who have been in your position can be inspiring. This will be a chance for your supporters to help spread your network. If they do not have the answer, they can put you in touch with someone in their network who knows. You now have a new person in your network, someone who is already impressed by your dedication and willingness to acquire new skills. This is how job offers suddenly appear for those who are well connected professionally.

2. Even if you are not a member, look at the websites of professional bodies in your target area to see what qualifications and training are expected. We would not recommend that you sign up to a course that a professional body is advertising without any further research, but we would urge you to use the website to get a good sense of what training or studying will give you an edge.

3. Look at job adverts and job descriptions – is there a recurring pattern of the type of qualification or professional development activity that is being indicated as desirable in the field? If enough employers want it, you had better go out and get it.

4. Colleges do more than just train – they also offer advice and guidance. If you are not sure that you want to commit to a course, or you are uncertain about your ability to undertake some training, you do not have to sit and worry about it. Just make an appointment to see a study advisor or course leader at your local college.

5. If you are receiving benefits you might see government agencies as existing to enforce the system, but actually they can also be a rich source of information and signpost you towards agencies (both centrally funded and locally supported) that could help you in your professional development and career planning. Go to www.gov.uk/career-skills-and-training for more on this.

EXERCISE #10: Would a portfolio career suit me?

Read through the following example of a portfolio career, which incorporates elements of both parallel and longitudinal careers:

Rebecca knew that she wanted to work abroad in order to learn about other cultures and she enjoyed teaching, so after university she taught English to children in France for three years. During this time she improved her cultural awareness, her communication skills, her planning and delivery of classes (presentation skills) and she enjoyed meeting new people. She also worked in a restaurant in the evenings so that she could afford to go off exploring the area every few weeks. She decided to return to the UK and put these transferable skills to good use by starting her new career as a manager in a large international business. She led conference calls liaising with teams around the world and ran several lucrative projects, leading her to develop her project management skills, her leadership skills and her understanding of budgets and the 'bigger picture' thinking required by her job.

Rebecca drew on her English degree as she had to write reports during this time. Her third dream career was running her own business organising sporting events for disadvantaged children. After some years of employment she chose to reduce her hours so she could work part-time and develop her own business at the same time. She now uses her business acumen to persuade large corporations to give donations to her clients, all of which are charities; she uses her communication skills to talk with managers, fund-raisers and families; her presentation skills are vital for engaging with large businesses; her negotiation and leadership skills have made her business a success. She now intends to set up offices in other countries and expand her business. Her long-term goal is to retire early so that she can go back to France and open her own restaurant.

1. What is your immediate emotional reaction to this example? Did it make you feel anxious because it all seemed so uncertain? Did the way her career changed make you feel exhausted by the thought of so much hard work and training? Or perhaps you felt excited by what she had done and envious of the life she had been able to create?
2. What is your more considered aspirational reaction to the story? Does it make you want to reach her sort of dream, or is yours quite different? Consider for a moment the ways in which your goals might coincide with, or differ from, Rebecca's goals. This will give you some clues as to whether this option might be for you.
3. Did one type of portfolio career (either parallel or longitudinal) appeal to you more than another? Maybe you enjoyed the idea of her teaching and working in a restaurant at the same time, but were less keen on the larger career changes? Or vice versa?
4. By now you might have discarded the idea of a portfolio career, in which case you need go no further. However, if you are intrigued by the idea, now is the time to ambush yourself. Without thinking about it in too much detail, list the different careers that might interest you and when in life you see yourself doing these. You might already be planning a career break, for example, or you might expect to be working past the standard retirement age, or perhaps you want to spend some years studying and working at the same time.
5. You have formed a draft plan of how a portfolio career might work for you – well done!
6. Leave the draft plan to one side for a few days and then return to it every now and then, each time just working on it for a while and then letting it sit for a time again. Portfolio careers can be amazing – we both love ours – but they take time and thoughtful preparation to make sure that they serve all of the functions you demand of them.

EXERCISE #11: Planning for a portfolio career

1. Using the exercise above, you will now have a list of the careers you would like to do.
2. Double check that they are all viable options for you (do not include mountain guide, for example, if you are actually a teeny bit scared of heights).
3. Now look at how much money you need to earn in order to feel secure.
4. Talk with those people you know who have a portfolio career so you get a good sense of how best to manage it.
5. Evaluate what each career requires in terms of qualifications and prior experience. This will help you establish which career(s) you can start immediately, and which you will need to work towards over some time.
6. Plan your 'get out'. This is your timescale for when you will move on to another career plan. You may choose to decide this by the length of time you want to commit to it or the skills or experiences you want to achieve before moving on. You should also consider how long you can financially afford to do this career, or how long you need to occupy this particular role in order to earn enough to secure the next stage of your career.
7. Plan how you will manage two or more careers at one time and remember to include time for marketing or liaising with people in your networks to ensure that you have the next job lined up and are always moving on to something. We also recommend that you include in your plan your leisure time as you will find yourself extremely busy and you cannot work efficiently or effectively when you are worn down, stressed and overwhelmed.
8. Keep your plan somewhere nearby so that you can refer back to it if you feel like you are starting to lose track.

Both of the exercises above are challenging and are going to take time and effort to complete. Use your networks so that you can talk your ideas through with your supporters, who will offer you reality checks as well as encouragement, and take your time. Planning time will not be wasted time when you are making such a major decision.

EXERCISE #12: Deciphering the career market and my career preferences

What we mean by brainstorming is simple – it is no more than a rapid sharing of ideas, without any judgement about what might be included in your final list of careers.

1. Sit down with a group of supporters (as many as possible) and have a large piece of paper in front of you.

Top tip

People are often flattered to be asked to do this, so you could invite people and make a special occasion of it.

2. Designate one person as 'the scribe', to jot down ideas as they emerge.

Top tip

The scribe needs to be a speedy writer and forceful enough as a character to tell everyone to keep quiet every now and again while the scribe catches up with the flow of ideas.

3. Write your name in a circle in the centre of the sheet of paper.

Top tip

Do not be mean spirited in this – use the largest possible piece of paper (the back of a roll of wallpaper, or the back of a poster, or a piece of flipchart paper) and large pens so that every idea stands out and looks decisive.

4. If you are working with mentors or professional contacts, they may need to know a little more about the skills you are offering and the areas of activity in which you excel, so you could put a list of these under your name in the centre, to offer people some direction.

Top tip

Your family and friends know you well, but this can be a problem at moments like these. They might reasonably assume that they know exactly which skills you want to use, or believe that you still excel in an area that you lost interest in years ago. Putting these notes in the centre will help your family and friends as much as your professional mentors and supporters.

5. You will need to start things off by suggesting a few careers that interest you. The scribe just writes these down anywhere on the piece of paper. Once you have produced these

few, invite others to join you by shouting out their ideas. By the end of the exercise you will have a very full and rather messy looking piece of paper with your future career somewhere in there.

Top tip

Do not be judgemental and do not try to order things too precisely in these early stages. Any idea is a good idea because, however off the mark it is, it could lead to a more suitable idea from another member of the group. Ideas are flung on the paper – any attempt to draw lines to connect these or order them in terms of preference will reduce the creative process.

6. Before you start, allocate one member of the group as 'the prompt'. The prompt says nothing whilst the ideas are flowing, but every time the ideas begin to dry up, the prompt will shout out an idea or two and this will help get ideas sparking again.

Top tip

It can be handy if the prompt has a laptop to hand so as to be researching careers whilst everyone else is shouting out ideas.

7. Once you have a brainstorm that feels complete, put this to one side for a while before you do anything more with it.

Top tip

If you can, arrange to have a number of brainstorming sessions with several entirely different groups of people; that way you will get the widest possible range of appealing careers ideas.

8. After you have taken some time away from your brainstorm, go back to it and be ruthless. Cross out every career idea that you know, deep down, is not the right one for you. Put a question mark beside any ideas that potentially appeal to you, but about which you would like to find out a bit more before you decide. Put a plus sign (+) beside any idea which is not ideal for you, but is still in enough of the right area that you would like to use it as a trigger for further discussion with your mentors.

Finally, put a very deliberate, thick circle around every career idea that is left. This is your starting point – congratulations!

Top tip

If you are not able to meet in person with all of your supporters, you can still brainstorm online, either by creating a document online and sharing with others, or via email and asking for just a few ideas from each supporter so you can transfer these to your own brainstorm sheet of paper.

EXERCISE #13: Once I know what I might want to do, how do I continue researching it?

1. When you come back to the lists, lay them out next to each other for easy comparison. Give yourself space to see all of these clearly.
2. Be firm and turn over any of the career sheets that you now believe to be unsuitable for you and tell yourself or your supporter/mentor why you feel like this. This will reinforce your decision if you say it out loud and will also give your supporter/mentor a chance to understand your reasoning and question it if they disagree.
3. Of those careers that are left, create fact sheets describing each job and talk them through with your supporter. Your supporter or mentor should be looking out for whichever one you speak most passionately about. They should also listen to the language choices you make as these can sometimes be very revealing about how you truly feel. For example, if you use 'it should' or 'I should' when describing a career, you still have mixed feelings about it and you may have to really explore who or what is making you feel like you *should* follow that career path. On the other hand, if you are using language such as 'really hope', 'want', 'wish', 'dream', then it would be reasonable to assume that you feel more positively toward this career. You may now be able to remove some more career options from your options pool.
4. Once you have narrowed down your career opportunities, you will need to think critically about each one. You will have already considered in Step One (see page 31) what your motivators are and what values you prioritise, so you should now use these to decide which career would suit you best. For example, if you value multiple training opportunities within a career, you may be able to identify which career could offer these now that you have done some research.
5. From those that are still face up in front of you, order your career research sheets in order of the most desirable career to the least desirable career for you. By now, even the least appealing should still be a perfectly good career for you.

You are now ready to take the next step of trying to get into your ideal career.

Remember!

You do not have to dismiss any of the careers that you have now identified as suitable for you; you may choose to have a portfolio career.

EXERCISE #14: What about cold calling on the phone?

1. Find a target organisation – one that has been advertising in your area of interest recently for example, or that has been doing something that has piqued your curiosity. Your networks can be really useful here in offering you details of organisations you might like to target.
2. Have your master CV beside you, printed out and with the areas you particularly want to talk about highlighted on it. The point of having your master CV rather than a highly targeted document beside you is that this could become a wide-ranging discussion, and you will want the material beside you to back up whatever you end up discussing.
3. Check online (or in any company literature you have been able to find) so as to find the best person to talk to in the first instance. You may prefer not to ask simply for the Personnel or Human Resources (HR) department – it could prove more productive to talk to a manager in the department in which you would actually like to work. How much work you put into gathering information before you make the call will depend on your level of enthusiasm for the organisation. If this is your dream company, you might want to ring up in advance to ask them to send you a company brochure or annual report. It makes sense not to go for your very top, ideal organisation for this first try.
4. Make sure that you are as ready for this call as you would be for a telephone interview (we discuss these in Step Seven, page 127) – you will want to make the best possible impression. One way to prepare is to block caller ID before you make the call. That way, you can just hang up and try again later if you get flustered in the first few seconds.
5. Ask the receptionist for the person you want to talk to and be sensitive to the response. If you find the receptionist surly or rude, and the person you speak to seems stressed and uninterested in your call, you might want to reconsider whether this is such an ideal organisation. It will not necessarily put you off completely, but you would be on your guard. If the person to whom you wanted to speak is not there, but you get a friendly response on the end of the phone from someone who works in the same department, use that contact and start your opening questions. If there is only one person you need to speak to and they are out of the office, never ask that you are called back. You are asking for a job here, so you need to be seen to be making the effort. If you do get through, the person you want to speak to may well be working under a time pressure, so always ask at the outset of the call whether your contact has time to talk to you for just a few minutes; if not, you would, of course, be happy to call back at a more convenient moment.

6. Opening with a closed question such as 'Do you have any vacancies?' is inviting just one of two responses, and if that response is 'No' then you have not made the most of the phone call. Instead, prepare a preamble in advance and go in softly so as to make this into a conversation which will, ideally, become a mini interview. Practise openings such as 'I was recently reading about your expansion into Europe and it has made me wonder whether you might have need of a colleague with languages skills. As a fluent speaker of Spanish … ' or 'I noticed last month that you were advertising for sales people. Sales is not my field, but your adverts were so appealing that it made me want to approach you directly to ask about any other opportunities … ' If you are feeling less bold about selling yourself, a more low-key opening might be 'I have been reading up about your organisation recently and I wonder if you could tell me if you have any vacancies in your department at the moment, or if you know where your organisation's vacancies are usually advertised?'

There are so many ways you might open this conversation, and what you say will depend on your circumstances; try asking your first question out loud to yourself (or a supporter) before you make the call to ensure that it is an open rather than a closed question (that is, a question that invites conversation rather than calling for a one-word answer). You will get braver and more adept at this as you go along. Most people are daunted by the idea of picking up the phone in these circumstances, but we have seen even very shy callers turn into expert salespeople for their own talent after just a few phone calls.

7. Switch from the phone to an online set-up at any stage if you think this would be an effective way forward. If, for example, you are told that vacancies are advertised in a particular online journal, or if it is clear that any link or information could be sent to you online, try to move to an email conversation by asking for an email address. That way you can take the initiative by emailing to thank your contact for an interesting conversation and asking for the links or material that were mentioned. Be ready to attach your CV to that first email if you believe that you have enough information in hand to target this effectively.

8. Make notes throughout and after the phone call, and write out clearly at the end of those notes exactly what you have agreed or planned to do next. We would encourage you to make a series of these calls in one sitting, and since it is easy to get confused about what you have said to whom a separate file for each organisation is a good idea, with the material you gathered before the call, the master CV you used with the points you discussed noted on there, the details of your contact and any other useful information you were offered, and a clear note on the top of your next action.

By the end of a session of, say, six calls, you will have some nice fat folders of information, notes for the action you are to take next, and a clear sense of direction and achievement. Have a treat ready for yourself after the first call – it is highly motivating to offer yourself even a small reward for being brave!

EXERCISE #15: How to cold call in person

1. Be dressed as if ready for an interview; if you are hoping to meet the person who could be employing you, making a great first impression is obviously going to be crucial. You might choose not to wear a suit, if the organisation is not a 'suit type of place', but you will need to carefully consider which outfit would give the right impression to your target organisation.

2. Have with you the details of any person you would like to speak to about possible openings. These could be job vacancies or perhaps volunteering or shadowing/placement opportunities: try to be open-minded about all the information you receive. If you write out the details of the person and/or the department you want to contact, you can make sure that you do not get too tongue-tied in those first few seconds, and there is no chance that you will get muddled on names; if you are not sure how to pronounce a name, having it in writing can be a relief to you and the person who first greets you when you enter the building.

3. Also have in your folder any material you have gathered about the organisation. You will probably not need to refer to this but it is a good idea to have it with you to help you keep your focus. You can skim through it one last time before you enter the organisation's premises. The very fact that you have this information demonstrates how committed you are to succeeding in your venture, so if there is any excuse to take this out and refer to it, take the opportunity to do so.

4. You might be asked to leave your CV rather than, or as well as, talking to someone, so make sure that, rather than the master CV you would use for a phone call, you have a targeted copy of your CV to hand for this moment. If you feel you cannot target your CV until you know more about the situation, be ready to email it after the event.

Simply leaving your CV at the front desk is only partway towards what you need to achieve. If you are very nervous, this might be the only step you feel you can take, and that is fine, but you will need to call later to make sure that the right person actually received your CV and you would hope then to have a discussion about potential prospects.

Top tip

Receptionists, especially if they are on temporary contracts and so new to a company themselves, can be extremely useful sources of 'inside information' about their company, so see the very first conversation you have when you walk into the building as a useful part of the process. Get chatting if you can and make a mental note of your impression of the place after that conversation.

5. When you speak to someone you will want to have an opening line or two that you have practised in advance, but try not be too rigid about what you want to say. It would be fantastic if they responded to your approach by telling you straightaway that there is a job on offer that is perfect for you, but it really is almost as good just to have made the contact. Any conversation you have will be useful: you are making another contact for your network, you are gathering valuable inside information, and you have actually met someone who has taken your CV.

EXERCISE #16: How much should I compromise?

1. Using the list of considerations below to guide you and adding more as you think of them, write the ones that are most important to you on one side of the scales. These should be the things that you absolutely cannot compromise on unless in extreme circumstances.
2. Above the middle of the scales, write all of the things that are not so important to you and you feel you can be flexible on.
3. You can now see that everything sitting on one side of the scales is really important to you and so you would need a large enticement or benefit from the employer to be able to be flexible on these. So, on the other side of your scales, write down what would make you compromise on these things.
4. Once you have this, you will know what you are willing to compromise on and feel more confident about what you are happy to accept. This means that when you go into nego-tiations with your employer, you do not end up walking away feeling that you have lost something.

Hours of work	Annual leave	Your own space at work (office, desk, etc.)
Salary	Childcare service	Regular pay reviews
Health insurance	Long/regular breaks	Maternity/paternity arrangements
Dental	Flexible hours	Unpaid leave policy
Bonuses	Autonomy	Team-building events
Rate of overtime pay	Managing your own projects	Commuting
Working from home	Career progression options	In-house training

EXERCISE #17: What if I am not offered the job after an interview?

Make a note of your responses to these questions, preferably before you receive any feedback from the organisation:

1. Did you turn up on time and greet your interviewer(s) well?
2. On reflection, do you think that you were dressed appropriately?
3. Did you make eye contact and smile at appropriate moments?
4. Did you prepare thoroughly enough?
5. Do you think that you gave full enough answers throughout, or would they have found it difficult to talk to you?
6. Were there any questions where you rambled in your answer or perhaps talked for too long?
7. Were there any questions that you struggled to answer? Write these down so you do not forget them.
8. Do you feel that you built up a good rapport with the interviewer(s)?
9. Did you manage to ask questions that gave you a further opportunity to sell your skills and stress your enthusiasm for the post?
10. Did you conclude the interview process professionally, shaking hands, smiling and making eye contact with the interviewer or each member of the interview panel?

EXERCISE #18: What if I have just accepted the wrong job?

1. Write down the reasons that you applied for the job in the first place. Do they still look like valid reasons to you?
2. List the reasons why you now believe this job to be the wrong one for you.
3. Talk to a friend or family member about your concerns as they may be able to allay your fears.
4. Sleep on it. Your brain utilises different areas when you are sleeping, so if you go to sleep worrying over a problem then you are likely to find an answer in your sleep that you would not have come up with whilst awake.
5. If you still believe that you have accepted the wrong job then you need to inform the organisation.

EXERCISE #19: What if I have started the job and now realise it is not suitable for me?

1. Complete the following table to look at all of the areas of the job.
2. Establish who or what can help you fix this.
3. Set a review date so that you have given yourself a timeframe in which the job should improve for you. This means that if it does not, you can decide whether there is any reason to continue in the job or whether it is best to look for a new one.

Area	What is the challenge?	How might I be able to fix it?	Who or what could help me?	Review date
Example: Work hours	*Working 9am–5pm means I get stuck in traffic*	*Start work at 8am and finish at 4pm*	*My line manager could authorise this*	*Two weeks' time*
Work hours				
Commute				
Colleagues				
Manager				
Workload				
Environment				
Technology				
Socialising at work				
Support				
Induction/ information				

This table offers a few of the most common reasons for second thoughts in a new career; you will probably want to add more features specific to your circumstances. It will help you plan a medium-term strategy, but you should also plan what you can do to help your situation in the meantime. Make sure that you utilise the intranet within your organisation to find out more about jobs or projects that come up. You could also talk with your manager about what else you would like to do in your work life as managers are often able to offer information about roles that are coming up in an organisation. Socialise with your colleagues during breaks so that you find out about internal opportunities and you will also find that your work becomes easier if you know who can assist you. Socialising also makes your work environment more interesting and hopefully much more fun.

EXERCISE #20: How do I build up a network?

1. For each of your networks, consider all of the contacts and then choose the two that you feel you can most easily approach.
2. Identify a specific way that each of the people you have identified might be able to help you further. This does not need to be an onerous task for either of you. It could be anything from offering you the contact details of someone they have heard of who has expertise in an area of interest to you, to introducing you by email to a colleague of theirs who could help and advise you. Success in this exercise depends upon you being able to find a specific need and then identifying the right person to help.

3. Contact those people and ask them if they could offer you the name of someone who could help you in the specific way you have identified, then make the next move and actually get in touch with that person.
4. Once you have the information you need, add that person to one of your networks. As long as you keep feeling the need to cover an area that is not yet fully supported by your existing network contacts, keep repeating this process with different contacts in each network.

EXERCISE #21: How do I maintain my networks?

1. Each week, check your networks – is everyone who should be in your networks actually on the list?
2. Every two weeks, check your online network – have you responded to requests to join social media network sites? Have you asked to link to useful people about whom you have heard recently? Has anything appeared unexpectedly on the internet that portrays you in a negative light?
3. Every three weeks, brainstorm your needs. Think about your current situation and what would help you most – make a list of your needs. Look at your networks and identify who could help and what you need them to do – make a list of people and actions and then contact them.
4. Each month attend an event that will help you professionally. This might be a conference, a social gathering, a training course – anything that will keep you in touch with the wider world.

EXERCISE #22: How can I make the most of a placement?

1. Be clear about exactly why you are going on placement (you will probably have several different reasons for doing it).
2. Consider first where you can reasonably go on placement. Whether you are arranging your own or being offered a variety of prearranged placements, you will need to think about the practicalities first.

Top tip

Where you can go on placement if you are studying at university will depend on when you are planning to undertake this, if you are studying away from home. If the placement is to be carried out in the vacation, a placement near your home address is clearly a better option from the point of view of transport.

3. Think about the type of situation that would suit your needs. Be as specific as you can in this, if you are clear about where you want to be. So, rather than just wanting to work for a publishing firm, ask yourself which department would suit you, or consider whether you would rather rotate through several departments.

4. Once you have the situation or situations listed, be open to some lateral thinking. List all of the organisations that might offer you a placement (or narrow down the list of pre-arranged placements to those that truly appeal to you), even if these are not obvious. Remember that large pharmaceutical firms have logistics departments, whilst huge multinationals have in-house reporters, and hospitals have publicity departments. You could boost your chances of getting a great placement if you are prepared to think imaginatively about where you want to be.

5. Now examine the list of placements you have produced by this point. Make sure that you have a good balance between large and small organisations, and those that are well-known compared to the lesser known organisations. It can be tempting only to apply for what you perceive to be glamorous, big-city placements for huge conglomerates, but this can sometimes mean rather a banal placement because there is little scope for flexibility in the system.

6. If you can, you also need a balance between those providers who have placements running all of the time and those for whom this is only the first or second time they have been involved in offering a placement. The former will have a well-tried placement structure, but the latter might offer you scope to mould your placement to your particular needs.

7. Once you have your final list of placement providers, having gone through steps 1–6 you may need to do nothing else but apply, if these are prearranged placements with activities already set up in advance. If you are approaching placement providers direct to craft your own sort of placement, it would help if you decided on the type of placement that appeals to you most:

   - A *shadowing* placement, where the person undertaking the placement would observe the activities of a professional and write a report on what has been observed and learnt as a result.
   - A *participation* placement, where the person undertaking the placement carries out day-to-day activities and then reports on the learning that has resulted from this.
   - A *project* placement, where the person undertaking the placement takes on a distinct, small project (or one part of a larger project) and reports on that whilst also reflecting on what has been learnt.

8. Having targeted your potential placement providers and, if you can, decided on the type of placement that appeals to you, make contact with the providers, keeping a clear idea of what you want to do and how this will be of benefit to them.

Remember!

This last point is crucial. You must match what you are asking for with what a placement provider needs. If you are mainly interested in experience of the workplace, then helping out around an office will provide what you want and what the provider needs; however, if you want to enhance your portfolio of material as a potential journalist, you will have to convince a provider that you can produce publishable copy during the placement. The benefit must always flow both ways.

9. As soon as you have reached this stage of clear-minded purpose, get on with it! Delay is the enemy of a good placement. Even if you are being offered prearranged placements it can take months to sort out the practicalities.

10. Keep the records you have produced from this exercise and make them the basis of your placement log. Whether or not you have to write up a formal reflection on your experience, keeping a record of what you have achieved and learnt on placement will help you maximise its benefits.

EXERCISE #23: What headings should I include in my CV?

Use this list to note down the points you might include in your CV. You will probably not include every point in every CV you produce, but it is useful to have all of these to hand. We have listed the areas of a CV under the headings that are most usually used, and in a fairly standard order, but the headings and order you use are up to you. If you prefer to foreground education over experience, for example, you might put that earlier.

Careful!

Before you begin on this exercise, remember our warnings about doing what you want to do, rather than what you think you should do. You can list everything here, but take a moment later to consider which items you might want to downplay. You would not want, for example, to highlight your fantastic telephone technique throughout your CV if actually you do not enjoy talking on the phone.

Name: This sounds so obvious, but put down the name you would like to hear as you walk into an interview room, so not perhaps your formal, registered name (although if your nickname is comic or cute, you might prefer more formality).

Contact details: Do not waste space giving your postal address line by line, but put it in one line across the page – you need every line you have got to make an impression. Similarly, they only need to know how to get hold of you to invite you to interview, so one email address and a phone number will do.

Careful!

If your email address is comic or a bit racy, set up an email account just for career purposes. If your mobile phone has a funny or overly casual answerphone message, smarten it up in case they call you. If you have an arranged time to call them or for them to call you, make sure that there is no chance of you being interrupted by friends or family during the call.

Key skills and experience: The reason you might include these, rather than launching straight into your education or work experience, is that you would want to impress upon the reader just how well suited you are to the job. By linking your list of four to six key skills/ experience areas to the job description and personal specification, you are making it very easy for them to select you.

Careful!

If all you do is list the key skills they are asking for, all you are proving is that you can read and copy very well! Make sure that, for each skill or piece of experience you mention, you can prove this and if possible show how it benefited a previous employer. So, rather than 'Customer Service: I have experience of customer service' you would write 'Customer Service: My response time to customer queries helped reduce complaints to my last employer by 19%' or 'Customer Service: I was praised for this aspect of my work in the restaurant in which I worked, with one diner calling me 'the most helpful waitress in the town'.

Education: List your qualifications and the courses you have undertaken, but list less recent qualifications along the line rather than down the page. That way you are not wasting space. If you feel that your professional development activities or your recent career experience are more important than your educational achievements, then put these above this section.

Professional development: Any course that you undertook at school, college or university that led to a nationally recognised educational qualification comes under 'Education'. Any training activity you have carried out beyond this, that is relevant to your professional life, is classed as a professional development activity. This could include some basic Health and Safety training, or a First Aid course, or some customer service training you undertook. Even a few hours of training counts here – it need not be an extensive or overly formal course.

Top tip

Professional development activity can be included on your CV even if you did not take an official course. If, for example, you spent a morning with your boss showing you how to answer the phone and handle clients in the call centre you worked in for a few weeks, this in-house training can (and should) be included on your CV.

Careful!

The first people in your target organisation to see your CV will not necessarily be the managers for whom you will work. The first sift through a pile of CVs might be carried out by people in the Recruitment Division or Human Resources. Indeed, a human being might not be involved at all if recognition software is used to discard those CVs that do not include key words or phrases. Make sure that your CV will make sense to a non-expert – avoid acronyms for any unusual qualifications or affiliations if you think these might not be recognised.

Career history: This section is sometimes called 'Employment History' (but does this sound as if you just want to be employed rather than aiming for a good career?) or 'Work Experience' (but does this suggest that you have never moved beyond the most basic experience?). 'Career history' tends to suggest a firm professional sense of identity.

Any job you have undertaken can be proudly included here. It does not matter in the slightest if it was not paid employment. Volunteering or working within a club or society is still part of the history of your career skills acquisition and professional experience. If it is relevant to what you are trying to say about yourself, include it.

Additional information: This is a flexible section, and might be split into several sections. You will want to include here the additional skills you have, perhaps the fact that you are fit and have a full, clean driving licence; if you speak another language that is not mentioned elsewhere, you might include it here. You might also want to include any hobbies and interests that you have (or you might include a separate 'Interests' section). You can also make a decision about whether you want to include your date of birth, nationality and/or national insurance number and/or permit number here.

Remember!

This is your CV, your sales pitch – you make the decisions. If you do not want to include personal information such as your date of birth, and you do not think that it will help your case, there is no need to do so.

References: Consider whether you need to include the full details of your referees. This will take up valuable space on your CV and is unlikely to sell you actively at this stage. You will also want to prepare your referees before they give the reference, by giving them a copy of your CV, the job description and person specification. Unless you know that, in your target industry, you would be expected to include their details here, you could use the space more effectively.

EXERCISE #24: How do I tackle open questions?

1. As you carry out research on the organisation, and scan the job description and/or person specification, note down the attributes, skills and experience that are required for the role. Begin to do this as soon as you start to think about applying, to give yourself plenty of time to contemplate.
2. As you work up this list, jot down, whenever a thought comes to mind, the ways in which you can prove that you have those skills and experience. Also (and this is often the more difficult task) write down how you can prove that you have the attributes required. This second part is as likely to call upon your experience outside the workplace as in it. Be bold about trumpeting your experience and/or success from all areas of your life.
3. From the list, select the six most important features they are looking for (these can come from skills, qualities or experience).
4. Put the list to one side for a time and then go back and quiz yourself – are these really the six features you believe are most important to the organisation?

Remember!

You have done much of this work if you have already produced skills and experience inventories.

5. Once you are happy with the list, go to the notes you made about what you are offering and write down, against each feature, an example that proves you fulfil that requirement, and wherever possible evidence that demonstrates how you have benefited an employer or succeeded in some way as a result of your abilities, experience or attributes.

So, for each feature, you will now have …

Requirement → Example/proof to show you can meet the need → Demonstration of how you have brought a benefit to a situation or employer in response to this requirement.

An example would be …

Customer Service → I was promoted in my last role after just six months because my dedication to customer service was recognised after I increased specialist sales in my area by 6%.

6. Lastly, work out how to set out your answer in the space given to you. If you are offered an online form that expands with your material and has no word limit, assume that this type of question will not require more than a one-page answer.

Remember!

You can take ownership of this process, even though you have to follow the instructions given to you on the form. Test out the features offered to you before you begin to fill out the form. If you can use bullet points, for example, you can make the open question page far more effective by structuring this around a clear list of concrete benefits you can offer.

EXERCISE #25: How can I stop myself panicking as I wait?

1. Sit down, place your feet flat on the floor and wiggle your toes. This should release any tension in your legs and make you feel a little calmer.
2. Put your hands gently on your thighs and spread out your fingers. This will make your hands, forearms and elbows relax.
3. Relax your tongue – bring it down from the roof of your mouth. This is a good time to take a sip of water if your mouth is dry.
4. Deliberately lengthen your neck, either by lowering your shoulders or by moving your head to position it perfectly over your spine.
5. Close your mouth and breathe out through your nose. Resist the temptation to breathe in until you are really desperate, then do not deliberately take a breath, but rather just open your mouth and let your diaphragm and intercostal muscles do the work. Rather than your shoulders tensing, you will find that you breathe from the very base of your chest.
6. Using your right arm, firmly pinch the top of your left shoulder, by your neck. Work along and then down the back of your left arm, pinching as you go until you get to your left wrist. This might feel quite uncomfortable if you are very tense, but it is an effective way

179

to release your neck, shoulder and arm muscles. Repeat using your left hand on the right side of your body.

7. Repeat this whole process three times. This will give you up to about seven minutes of artificially induced calm – more than enough for you to get into your interview stride.

EXERCISE #26: How do I prepare for an interview presentation?

If you are precise about the purpose of each rehearsal of your presentation, you will be able to move forward with purpose:

1. Rehearsal One: Read from a script or very detailed prompt cards, just to get a sense of the timing. You need not use your presentation aids at this point, but leave a pause for when you would look with your audience members at the screen, or show them something.

After this rehearsal, cut down or add to your presentation to make it perfect for time.

2. Rehearsal Two: Read from your revised script or reworked prompt cards to confirm that you now have the timing right.

After this rehearsal, make a set of sparse prompt cards (no more than few points per card) and throw your script away. From now on, just use the prompt cards.

3. Rehearsal Three: Rehearse using your new prompt cards, forcing yourself to keep going even if you stumble or feel lost every now and then.

After this rehearsal, make sure that your presentation aids are ready to go and your prompt cards are brief enough so that you do not read them like a script.

4. Take a break: You will need time to assimilate what you have achieved already and to make sure that you do not start to sound bored.
5. Rehearsal Four: Rehearse with prompt cards and presentation aids. In this practice you will be thinking about how effectively your presentation aids are working to support your presentation. You will know this well enough by now to be able to make a good judgement.

After this rehearsal revise your presentation aids to make them perfect.

Top tip

Tiny little errors on a presentation slide will become huge when they are up on a screen and your audience is staring at them for some time. Make sure that you proofread meticulously!

6. Rehearsal Five: use this practice to really boost your confidence – the presentation should now have taken shape in your mind.

Last minute changes will come after this rehearsal – the most useful thing you can do is to cut down your prompt cards so that they show just prompt words or phrases, with a few facts and figures. You might even decide to use what is on the screen as your only prompt.

7. Rehearsal Six: save this rehearsal until the day before the event, or the day itself, and run through it once without stopping to remind yourself of the whole package.

After this rehearsal do nothing more: you have your presentation ready and any more practising puts you in danger of sounding over-rehearsed and stale. You have done everything you need to do for success.

EXERCISE #27: What should I do when attending a recruitment/ job fair?

1. Find out, from the event advertising brochure and/or online, which organisations will be attending.
2. DO NOT DISMISS ANY OF THESE FROM YOUR PLANS YET!
3. Find out what roles each of them is trying to fill – let yourself be surprised. Put on a target list any that seem to have a role that is even close to what you would like to do.
4. Find out what skills they need, and what type of person they are looking for (if they are saying 'all subjects needed' rather than narrowing it down to just one area, they must know that they have a need for you). Add more organisations to your list based on their skills requirements.
5. Now gain an overview of the companies you have not listed (do a quick internet search for those you do not know) and see if you like the look of any of them. If you do, add these to your list. Even if they are not recruiting in your area of expertise at the moment they will be in the future, so having a conversation with them now is a good idea.
6. For each organisation on your list, write down three things that appeal to you about them (back to the internet for this, perhaps) and four things that you think will make you appealing to them. Take these lists with you as prompts on the day, along with copies of your CV.

181

Index